MW01640305

50 Years.
One Heart.

A History of Southwest in 50 Objects

Southwest®

To the one-of-a-kind Employees and loyal Customers of Southwest Airlines who made these first 50 years possible and who will inspire the next 50 … and beyond.

First Edition
ISBN: 978-1-882771-04-2
Library of Congress Control Number: 2021911714

Produced by History Factory
Washington, DC; Chicago, IL; Chantilly, VA
historyfactory.com

Published by Southwest Airlines
2702 Love Field Drive
Dallas, TX 75235
southwest.com

Contents

Foreword

By Gary Kelly

To say the past couple of years have been challenging is like saying the Hundred Years' War was a neighborhood squabble. (I dedicate that historical reference to our late Founder, Herb Kelleher, who, I'd like to think, is laughing uproariously at it.)

The COVID-19 pandemic and its aftermath has been a crisis unlike any this Company has seen, and we've been through the Great Recession, the 9/11 terror attacks, and repeated threats to our existence from competitors throughout our history.

We've persevered, but it hasn't been easy. The fact that you're reading this is also proof that we survived. Once again, we rose to the challenge. A new generation of Southwest Employees met this latest existential threat with the same vigor, determination, and loving support for each other that their forebearers demonstrated 50 years ago.

And that's why we want to take this opportunity to pause for celebration. Times are tough, and it might seem frivolous to write a book about ourselves, but in fact, this is precisely the time—not to toot our own horn, but to remember and reflect. We've overcome existential threats before, and we will again.

Besides, celebrations are part of what we do. We're a Company that celebrates the little things and the big things. We celebrate our People's birthdays, their children's graduations, weddings, promotions—almost anything you can imagine. And we celebrate corporate milestones.

But this corporate milestone is special—50 years of operations. How could we make this celebration special? Well, one way is the book you're reading.

Our Company was built on great stories, but we didn't want this book to bog down in the minutiae of every tale. We wanted it to be like us—lean and efficient—yet still hold true to its mission of capturing the richness of our first half century.

We decided on something a little different. We chose 50 objects from throughout our history, and we wrote stories about each one. The idea was to give readers a comprehensive overview of who we are and where we came from. Of course, we had to leave some stories out, which may have been the hardest decisions in the whole process.

This book highlights some of the most important, the most interesting, and the most pride-inspiring stories in our history. Some you may have heard before, and some may be new. We worked to tell even the most familiar tales in new ways, and I think you'll find we dug out a few details you may not have known. I know I learned a few things.

Most important, though, I hope you'll find that this book provides a richer understanding of our Company—why we did the things we did, and how the best Employees anywhere made those things possible. In fact, even though this is a book structured around objects, I think you'll find that many of these stories are really about the extraordinary People of Southwest Airlines. After all, this is their story. And this book is a tribute to the Company they built and continue to build.

What you'll find on these pages are stories of People and innovations, as well as examples of Southwest People connecting with Customers. You'll see how those factors combined to create a Company that has thrived in the face of overwhelming odds—and one that overcame all the naysayers. I think you'll see what has made Southwest not only a Company that redefined air travel in the past, but one that continues to be a defining force for the future as well.

I hope my successors running the Company 50 years from now—in 2071—can look back on their tenure with the same joy, pride, and love that I have for my time at Southwest Airlines. As I write this, I find myself wondering what Southwest will be doing in 50 years. I'm sure a lot will change—"Mars for less Moola! $59 each way!" "Venus for Vacation!"—but I hope it will still be a Company that puts its People first and believes in connecting Customers with what matters most in their lives.

As you'll see in these pages, that's what we've always done. And if we stay true to our Values, we'll continue doing it for another 50 years, regardless of the challenges.

We do that, as Herb said years ago, "by remembering at all times that what we do at work each day, each in our individual way, is part of a great crusade, and of a magnificent cause." We have never forgotten that. We are still fighting for our People and our Customers. And may we always be.

Ready for Takeoff

Southwest Earns Its Wings

A Lawyer, a Pilot, and a Crazy Idea Walk into a Bar …

It sounds like the setup to a joke, but it turned out to be the most important business meeting in the history of commercial aviation. By now, the "napkin story" has been told so many times that even many Customers can recite it by heart. But it bears retelling because every story has a beginning, and this is Southwest's.

It all started with a cocktail napkin and a hastily drawn route map. Commercial aviation would never be the same.

Rollin W. King, a Cleveland native, moved to Texas in 1962 after earning a Master of Business Administration degree from Harvard and began working as an investment banker. In 1964, two years before the famous napkin drawing (more on that in a bit), Rollin, a pilot, bought Wild Goose Flying Service (officially registered as Southwest Airlines, Inc.) in San Antonio, which flew charter flights with turboprop Beech 18s to Uvalde, Brackettville, and Eagle Pass—mostly for businessmen on hunting trips.

By 1966, the former Wild Goose was struggling. Rollin, realizing that Wild Goose would never lay the proverbial golden egg, asked his lawyer in San Antonio, Herbert D. Kelleher, to liquidate the company.

Dallas
Houston
San Antonio

Herb was a New Jersey native who had studied English literature and philosophy at Wesleyan University in Connecticut and then earned a degree from the New York University School of Law. He clerked for the New Jersey Supreme Court and then joined the state's largest law firm, working in corporate law before moving to San Antonio to join the firm of Matthews, Nowlin, Macfarlane & Barrett.

Even then, Herb was a maverick who didn't believe in conventional wisdom. The way he looked at it, "If it's conventional, it ain't wisdom, and if it's wisdom, it ain't conventional." He worked furiously, frequently well into the night. He wrote legal briefs by hand on yellow tablets, which were piled on the floor in his office.

Even as Herb was working on the liquidation, Rollin, who had the heart of an entrepreneur, became convinced the problem was one of scale. His banker had just complained to him that it was too hard to drive between Texas' biggest cities. Why wasn't there a commuter airline in a state as big as Texas? What if, Rollin wondered, they flew bigger planes between the major cities of Texas?

Herb thought he was crazy, but he agreed to discuss the idea over a drink at the St. Anthony Club. Rollin had drawn inspiration from research by a local banker, and he'd been studying intrastate carriers in California, which, like Texas, is a sprawling state with long driving times between its big urban centers.

Pacific Southwest Airlines was having success in the intrastate California market, fueled by a booming economy and the fact that driving between that state's major cities took too long for many travelers. The idea seemed simple—low fares and reliable, frequent service between the state's major markets. Rollin was convinced it would work. Herb wasn't so sure.

At some point during the conversation, Rollin drew a triangle on a cocktail napkin, outlining the proposed route network—Dallas, Houston, and San Antonio. An airline that concentrated on those three cities just might work, he insisted. Herb still had doubts, but always the big thinker, he also recognized that such an airline could spur the economies of all three cities, which, in turn, would increase demand for more air travel.

While Rollin made a strong case for the new venture, they both realized that to make this work, they would need money.

"Where will we get the capital?" Herb asked.

"Capital? Oh, I guess we'll have to raise it," Rollin responded. Finally, Herb said,

"Rollin, you're crazy. Let's do it."

Herb and Rollin put in some of their own money and got Herb's brother-in-law Alfred Negley and John Peace, a lawyer and politician, to pitch in some seed capital as well. Initially, they decided they needed to raise another $250,000 in a private offering, but Herb, knowing that launching a new airline would likely be a fight, decided to double the amount. Ultimately, they raised $543,000.

Rollin and Herb both took active roles in the venture. Rollin was the first President at the airline's beginning and then served as Executive Vice President of Operations during the Company's first four years of flying. He remained a member of the Board of Directors for 39 years, until his retirement in 2006. He was also a Captain and the first name on the Pilot seniority list.

Herb initially served as General Counsel and Corporate Secretary. He became Chairman in 1978, a title he would

hold for 30 years. He also served as CEO and President, first in 1978 and then again from 1981 to 2001. He then relinquished his executive duties but remained Chairman until 2008, and the Board bestowed on him the honorary title of Chairman Emeritus. He maintained an office and a regular presence at the Company until his death in 2019. More important, he became the face of Southwest Airlines and an inspiration to tens of thousands of Employees.

The meeting—and the napkin—changed the course of commercial aviation. The Company that resulted would eventually dominate the skies not just over Texas but the nation. The famous cocktail napkin was lost to posterity, but Herb kept a re-creation of it framed in the boardroom.

Less than a year after Rollin sketched his vision for the future on a napkin, he formally incorporated the new company as Air Southwest Co., on March 15, 1967. With the money from the private offering, Herb filed an application with the Texas Aeronautics Commission on November 27, 1967, for "Air Southwest Co." Then all hell broke loose.

↑ Herb Kelleher, left, and Rollin King in 1970.

← Southwest Marketing Sales Representatives surprised Texas motorists who saw them piloting the airline's fleet of seven quirky vehicles painted in Southwest's livery.

COMMISSION
CHAIRMAN
HARRY P. WHITWORTH
VICE-CHAIRMAN
REX C. CAUBLE
SECRETARY
HUGH A. FITZSIMONS, JR.
MEMBERS
LUCIEN FLOURNOY
PAUL M. FULKS, SR.
JAMES LUTHER

DIRECTOR
CHARLES MURPHY

MAILING ADDRESS
P. O. BOX 12607
CAPITOL STATION
AUSTIN, TEXAS 78711

TELEPHONE
AC 512 475-4768

TEXAS AERONAUTICS COMMISSION

CERTIFICATE OF PUBLIC CONVENIENCE AND NECESSITY
NUMBER 22

AIR SOUTHWEST CO., doing business as AIR SOUTHWEST

is hereby authorized to operate as an intrastate common carrier by air for the transportation of persons and property, utilizing Federal Aviation Agency certificated aircraft of any gross take-off weight and subject to the conditions hereinafter set forth, the laws of the State of Texas and the requirements, rules and regulations of the Texas Aeronautics Commission, issued pursuant thereto, as follows:

Between and among the points Dallas/Fort Worth, Houston and San Antonio, Texas.

The service hereby authorized is subject to the following conditions:

The holder of this Certificate may begin or terminate, and begin and terminate, service at any airports serving those points named herein.

This Certificate shall be effective as of February 20, 1968.

IN WITNESS WHEREOF, the Texas Aeronautics Commission has caused this Certificate to be executed by the Director of the Commission, and the seal of the Commission to affixed hereto, as of the 20th day of February, 1968.

Signed and entered this the 6th day of November, 1970.

Charles Murphy
Charles Murphy, Director

OFFICES: SUITE 1104, STATE FINANCE BLDG., 111 EAST 17TH ST., AUSTIN, TEXAS

Certifiable

Applying for a certificate to start flying touched off a four-year legal battle that almost put an end to the airline before it started.

In 1967, when Herb arrived at a hearing of the Texas Aeronautics Commission (TAC) to consider Southwest's application, he found representatives of Braniff International Airways, Trans-Texas Airlines, and Continental Airlines—some of the biggest carriers operating in the state at the time—already there, ready to voice their opposition to a new airline.

Part of TAC's purpose was issuing operating certificates for intrastate airlines, which was partly why Rollin King was so eager—the state was basically asking someone to start a commercial airline in Texas.

TAC commissioners brushed aside the concerns of the other airlines and unanimously voted in February 1968 to grant an operating certificate for intrastate air service between Dallas, Houston, and San Antonio. (The airlines that argued against the certificate all had interstate operating certificates issued by the Civil Aeronautics Board [CAB] in Washington, D.C., prior to the Federal Aviation Administration [FAA] having a role in that process.)

The next day, the three opposing airlines convinced a federal district judge to issue a temporary restraining order, which put the TAC certificate on hold and triggered a legal battle that would go on for four years. "I was aware there was going to be a fight, and it was going to be a prolonged fight," Herb said. "But it turned out to be a much longer vendetta than I had anticipated."

The first courtroom battle dragged out for six months. At one point, a Braniff lawyer asked one of Southwest's key witnesses to speak up. The witness explained he couldn't because his collar was too tight. He had to borrow a shirt after Braniff lost his luggage.

Six months after the other carriers filed their lawsuit, the court ruled in their favor. The main cities of Texas were already served sufficiently by other airlines and didn't need a new carrier, the judge decided. Air Southwest appealed the ruling, and in March 1969, the Texas Court of Civil Appeals voted 2-1 to uphold the lower court decision. Strike two—but Herb was ready for another swing. The Company's Board of Directors, however, wasn't so sure.

This time, Herb appealed to the Texas Supreme Court and took stock of the airline's bleak situation: no airplanes or financial backers and more liabilities than cash.

A Board meeting was scheduled, and several Directors said it was time to face reality and dissolve the Company. Air Southwest was done before it ever got off the ground.

"Gentlemen," Herb said, rising to his feet, "let's go one more round with them. I will continue to represent the Company in court, and ... pay every cent of legal costs out of my own pocket." There were a few gasps, and then stunned silence. After more discussion, the Board decided to let Herb proceed.

Herb was an eloquent appellate attorney. He had, after all, clerked for the New Jersey Supreme Court. But he outdid himself that day, even impressing lawyers for the other side. The justices ruled unanimously to overturn the lower court rulings and allow the TAC to issue an operating certificate.

↑
Lamar Muse, left, Colleen Barrett, Rollin King, and Herb Kelleher after a court proceeding in 1973.

The other airlines appealed to the U.S. Supreme Court, which declined to hear the case in December 1970.

Air Southwest was back in business—but the fight was far from over.

In Houston, Lamar Muse, a veteran of five airlines, read a newspaper story about the court's decision. He called Rollin to congratulate him on the victory, and Rollin offered him the job running Air Southwest.

The Company began assembling its fleet and preparing to finally get off the ground. Air Southwest changed its name back to the one Rollin had used when he bought Wild Goose—Southwest Airlines. Service was set to begin on June 18, 1971, with a flight from Dallas Love Field to San Antonio, but the airlines that had lost in court weren't done yet.

Two days before Southwest's first flight, the CAB rejected a new complaint from Braniff and Trans-Texas (which had become Texas International) claiming Southwest might violate its limits on flying out of state. The fight still wasn't over, though. The other airlines convinced the Texas state court to again issue a restraining order preventing Southwest from flying.

The fledgling carrier was so close to operating that it was already doing test runs with empty planes. Herb jumped onto one of the jets at Love Field and asked the pilot to drop him off in Austin on the way to San Antonio. Herb raced to the Texas Supreme Court and convinced the justice who had written the earlier opinion in Southwest's favor to call an emergency hearing for the next day—June 17. "I do not know how he did that, but I have it on good authority that on the evening of June 16, 1971, Herb could be seen in a dark bar in a private club just off Congress Avenue in Austin, surrounded by an unusually large number of Supreme Court justices," Ron Ricks, Southwest Vice Chairman at the time, said at Herb's memorial service in 2019.

The next day, Herb made an impassioned argument that Southwest Airlines should exist. The court issued a temporary restraining order that prevented the lower court from enforcing the earlier order. "Absent that ruling, no flights would have occurred on June 18, 1971, and likely there would be no Southwest flights today," Ron said.

On June 18, 1971, Southwest's first commercial flight left the runway at Dallas Love Field, headed to San Antonio, piloted by Emilio Salazar and Bob Pratt.

"I think my greatest moment in business was when the first Southwest airplane arrived after four years of litigation," Herb later recalled.

"I walked up to it, and I kissed that baby on the lips and I cried."

The legal struggles weren't over. Almost every time Southwest would expand service or enter a new city in those early years, one of its competitors would sue or complain to the CAB. They didn't realize they had already lost.

"I have often said that if Braniff and Texas International had left us alone and not been so rotten and dirty and tried to sabotage us every step of the way, Southwest Airlines would not be in business today," Herb said years later. "The more dirty tricks they played, the more resolved I became to beat them."

The Plane

Founder Rollin King's original plan for Southwest Airlines included buying three Lockheed L-188 Electra turboprops to fly four daily round trips between Dallas and Houston, two between Dallas and San Antonio, and one between San Antonio and Houston.

Southwest found one type of aircraft that would serve the Company through its first 50 years and beyond.

"You've got to be kidding!" then-President Lamar Muse said when he saw the plan. He knew that most passengers wouldn't want to fly on turboprops if competitors were offering jet service.

But the legal battle for survival had left the Company with almost no money. It had $142 left in the bank and some $80,000 in unpaid bills. On a gamble, Lamar flew to San Diego to observe Pacific Southwest Airlines (PSA), the carrier Rollin had used as a template in developing his plan for Southwest. PSA was flying Boeing's new 737-200s. He soon learned that, because of the recession, Boeing had several "white tail" 737-200s built on spec for airlines that later refused delivery. Unfortunately, Boeing wanted more than Southwest was willing to pay.

SOUTHWEST
Southwest
N8667D
SOUTHWEST

So, Lamar and Rollin flew to Long Beach, California, to meet with executives at Douglas Aircraft, who were interested in selling some DC-9-30s, the dominant short-range passenger jet at the time. But Lamar was drawn to the 737, in part because few other airlines seemed interested in them. On the drive from the airport, he scratched out some purchase conditions on a yellow legal pad.

When they arrived at Douglas' headquarters, Lamar went to a pay phone in the lobby and called Boeing. He told Boeing's head of domestic sales that he was meeting with Douglas to negotiate the purchase of three DC-9s. He read off the conditions he'd written on the legal pad and gave the Boeing executive an hour to make a counteroffer.

The meeting with Douglas was barely underway when the Boeing salesman called back and accepted Lamar's terms—three 737s with an option for a fourth for a total price of $4 million, no money down, and payments of $50,000 a month per aircraft for 60 months.

Southwest now had planes, but the first year remained a struggle, and the Company reported a net loss of $3.7 million. About three months after service began, the carrier received its fourth 737 under Lamar's deal with Boeing and used the new plane to start service at Houston's Hobby Airport. In May 1972, after yet another court ruling in yet another lawsuit by Braniff had kept Southwest from flying interstate charters, the Company sold one of the original planes to Frontier Airlines to raise much-needed cash.

From then on, the fleet grew, and by the end of the decade, Southwest was operating 16 planes and had placed an order for nine more. The Company was on its way to becoming a Texas icon, and its original "desert gold" livery and frequent flights earned it the nickname "the brown bus."

By early 1980, Southwest had expanded its fleet even more, and a large order of jets was being considered by the new President and CEO, Howard Putnam. (Lamar Muse had left the Company in 1978, replaced briefly by Founder Herb Kelleher until Howard, a United Airlines veteran, was hired.) By then, the Company had realized that maintaining one aircraft type was essential to its low costs. It saved money on maintenance because it needed to stock only one set of parts, and it gained training efficiency because Pilots, Flight Attendants, and Mechanics needed to learn only one set of procedures. These savings would become a huge competitive advantage. But the 737-200 was in desperate need of an upgrade—it had been introduced in 1967, the same year Southwest incorporated—and the Company needed planes with more seating.

"We asked if Boeing would consider upgrading the current 737 and learned they had been thinking about doing so for quite some time, but no airline had shown any interest," Howard said.

"We convinced them that our interest was sincere and immediate. Within three months, Boeing presented us full specs on a stretched 737. It was called the 737-300, and it was just what Southwest needed."

↑
Rollin King, left, and Lamar Muse stand in front of one of three original 737-200s before Southwest Airlines began operations on June 18, 1971.

The 737-300 that Howard ordered, now known as part of the Classic generation, was a big step forward from its predecessor and far quieter to operate, which became another competitive advantage. The planes cost $16.2 million each, and Southwest ordered 10 of them. "It was a bet-the-Company investment," Vice Chairman Ron Ricks said. "[We wanted] quiet airplanes specifically to be able to go into communities and say, 'By adding flights, we're actually not going to be adding noise. These airplanes are so much quieter.' It turned out to be one of the best things we ever did." The first 737-300 entered service in December 1984.

Despite Southwest's allegiance to the 737, the Company has operated other aircraft for short periods, such as leased 727s in its early years, the 717 after it acquired AirTran, and the McDonnell Douglas DC-9s after Southwest bought Muse Air and renamed it TranStar.

By the late 1980s, Southwest was big enough it didn't have to augment its fleet with other models. In 1987, the Company placed an order for the next variant of the plane, the 737-500, and in 1993, it announced it would be the launch customer for the 737X (which became the 737-700) with a commitment to purchase 63 jets through 2001. The first 737-700 arrived on December 17, 1997, and two years later, Southwest took delivery of its 300th 737.

Southwest's commitment to the 737 has never wavered, even after 9/11, when most other carriers canceled new jet orders. "Boeing said the only way they kept the assembly line open on the 737 ... was because Southwest agreed to take airplanes we couldn't even fly, to fulfill our contractual obligations to Boeing," Ron said.

While the airline continued to order more of the planes—its fleet topped 400 in 2004—it also retired some of the older workhorses from the early days. The last 737-200 model was retired from service in 2005. A year later, the 737 became the best-selling commercial jet of all time, and Southwest, with almost 450 737s by then, operated more of them than anyone in the world—which is still true today.

The 737 continued to evolve, and in 2010, Southwest announced it would introduce the 737-800 to its fleet. A year later, it committed to launching the next variant, the 737 MAX. The first Southwest 737-800 entered service in 2012, and the first MAX arrived in 2017.

Chairman and CEO Gary Kelly recently reflected on Southwest's long history with the 737: "The airplane is, I think, the best in the world," he said. "We've been delighted with it."

GOODYEAR

Turning on a Dime

Southwest Teams had just 10 minutes to "turn" a plane when it arrived at the gate—get it provisioned and fueled, get Passengers boarded, retract the jet bridge, pull up the wheel chocks, and get it back in the air.

Southwest Airlines' ability to turn an airplane around at the gate in just 10 minutes is a hallmark of its history, almost as legendary as the hot pants its Hostesses (now called Flight Attendants) used to wear. Back then, no one thought it was possible to turn a plane between flights with the speed and precision of a professional racing pit crew. No one, that is, except Bill Franklin.

Bill was a member of the "Over the Hill Gang," a group of seasoned airline veterans that Southwest's first President, Lamar Muse, hired in March 1971. The "gang" also included Don Ogden, Dick Elliott, and Jack Vidal. Bill had previously worked for Texas International and had taken a job with an airline in Denver, but he was anxious to return to Texas when Lamar approached him about a job. "I was equally anxious for a good ground operations officer, and, as far as I was concerned, Bill was the best there was," Lamar said.

In the spring of 1972, Lamar called a staff meeting for Pilots, Flight Attendants, Mechanics, and Station Personnel. He had a grim message: Southwest was bleeding cash. About six months earlier, the Company had added a fourth airplane to enable hourly service between its three cities—a competitive gamble the Company hoped would pay off. The airline also hoped to use the fourth plane to offer interstate charters.

↑
A Southwest Mechanic helps prepare a plane at the gate at Dallas (Love Field) as Provisioning Agents service the rear galley in the winter of 1971-1972.

Founder Rollin King originally studied the operations of Pacific Southwest Airlines as a business model, and it scheduled 25 minutes from the time a plane arrived until it departed on the next flight. Southwest did the math. The flight time from Dallas to both Houston and San Antonio was 50 minutes. If Southwest allowed 25 minutes between flights, it could offer service only every hour and 15 minutes. However, with a fourth aircraft, it could provide hourly service in the Dallas-Houston market (even if it was only averaging 17 Passengers per flight).

The fourth jet entered service on October 1, 1971, but things didn't go as planned. The hourly service didn't attract more Customers as was hoped, and the charter service was blocked by yet another Braniff lawsuit. Lamar made a deal to sell the fourth plane for about $4 million.

But before he went through with the deal, he needed to know if Southwest could still offer hourly service with just three planes. Since the flight times were fixed, the only option was reducing the time the plane spent on the ground between flights. Could Southwest's People, he asked, turn a plane in 10 minutes?

The response: "We can, and we will!" Not only did they do it, Southwest's ontime performance actually improved. "It was a Team effort, led by Bill Franklin," Lamar said.

The Over the Hill Gang may have been industry veterans, but most of the Frontline Employees weren't. That made it easier for them to do what seemed impossible.

"Most of us, not having an airline background, had no idea we couldn't do this, so we just did it," said Dennis Lardon, who was a Station Manager in San Antonio in 1973.

The 10-Minute Turn was born of necessity, of the need to transport the same number of Customers with three airplanes instead of four. But it came to epitomize a determination that today Southwest defines as its Warrior Spirit.

Howard Putnam, who was hired as President and CEO in 1978, later wrote, "What the Company did not immediately realize was that the 10-minute turnaround would also serve as a powerful motivator that inspired people to reach unexpected levels of productivity."

Several years later, Howard ordered a study to determine how much the 10-Minute Turn had saved. It found that Southwest would need three additional 737s to transport the same number of people if it had kept the standard 25-minute turnaround. "Southwest saved $6 million annually in interest alone—not to speak of the $60 million that the three [additional] jets would have cost," Howard wrote. In fact, turnaround time became vital to the Company's financial success, and for years it was cited as a critical business factor in its filings with the Securities and Exchange Commission.

"That was the single event that turned Southwest from a money-losing entity to a money-making entity," said Bob Montgomery, who started as a Ramp Agent in Lubbock in 1977 and rose to become Vice President Airport Affairs before retiring in 2020.

"People did not think it was possible," Vice Chairman Ron Ricks recalled. "The hardcore operating Employees in that Culture [brought] an airplane in, unloaded it, refueled it, reloaded it, put the Passengers on, and pushed it back in 10 minutes. Think about that. It's astounding how they did that. That was operationally driven, and it took a real operator to do that and maintain a high level of Customer Service in the process."

Eventually, changing regulations, larger planes, more carry-on bags, Southwest's entry into more congested airports, and security requirements made the 10-Minute Turn truly impossible, but the airline still has some of the best turn times in the industry, and the spirit of innovation that started with the 10-Minute Turn continues to this day.

↓

A Ramp Agent directs a 737-800 to a smooth stop at Houston (Hobby) in the summer of 2017.

When Wright Was Wrong

Love Field, Dallas' close-in airport, is more than just Southwest's home base. It's infused in Southwest's DNA. It's where the Company started its operations, and the airport's name is reflected in the Company's stock symbol, LUV, and its Heart logo. But Love Field was also the scene of one of Southwest's biggest threats and longest-running legal battles for survival. It all started before the Company's first jet ever took to the skies.

Four years after Herb had successfully established the airline's legal right to fly, he quickly found himself facing a new challenge. This time, the attack came from the cities of Dallas and Fort Worth, who were creating the new Dallas/Fort Worth Regional Airport (DFW). As part of the agreement between the cities and bondholders who financed the project, all commercial traffic was supposed to move to the new airport when it opened in 1974.

When Congress tried to limit flights from Love Field, Southwest launched a massive petition drive in opposition, boxing up thousands of them in shipping crates and sending them to Washington.

WRIGHT
IS WRONG

50,000
PETITIONS

WRIGHT
IS WRONG

Since Southwest wasn't even flying when the deal was made, it wasn't a party to it and had no intention of moving. The cities filed suit, and some of Southwest's old adversaries, including Braniff, joined them. Once again, Herb's legal prowess saved the day.

"If a three-aircraft airline can bankrupt an 18,000-acre, nine-miles-long airport, then that airport probably should not have been built in the first place," he told the judge.

The judge agreed. Southwest could stay at Love. And although the cities appealed, the appeals court ruled in the Company's favor in 1977, and the decision was sealed when the U.S. Supreme Court refused to hear the case.

Southwest had won the battle, but the war was just getting started. In 1979, with the ink barely dry on the year-old federal airline deregulation law, Southwest applied to the soon-to-be-dissolved Civil Aeronautics Board (CAB) for permission to fly outside of Texas for the first time—to New Orleans. Not surprisingly, some of the Company's major competitors once again objected, but this time they had an ally in Congress in Jim Wright, the House Majority Leader. Wright, who represented Fort Worth, supported moving commercial flights to DFW.

Southwest responded by organizing a massive petition drive, boxed up thousands of them in shipping crates, and delivered them to Washington in rented moving vans. Herb once again prevailed, with the CAB ruling that Southwest could, indeed, enter the New Orleans market.

But Wright wasn't done. He took the issue to the House floor and in one day got Congress to ban all interstate flights out of Love Field. Once again, Herb jumped into lawyer mode, calling on an old friend from law school, Bob Packwood. Packwood, a Senator from Oregon, was in line to lead the Senate Finance Committee.

While he didn't defeat Wright's law, Packwood forced a compromise: Southwest could fly from Love Field to the five contiguous states. The Company's biggest rivals, Braniff and American, which had moved its home base to DFW from New York, signed off on the deal. The Wright Amendment was born as a relatively small passage within a massive bill officially known as the International Air Transportation Competition Act of 1979.

↓
Colleen, riding to the top of Headquarters in a cherry picker, hangs a "WRIGHT IS WRONG" banner on July 27, 2005, as part of Southwest's efforts to repeal the Wright Amendment.

Employees at Headquarters gather under a banner celebrating the end of the Wright Amendment era on October 13, 2014.

Herb would later say that the legislation was a "pain in the ass," but it was one Southwest learned to live with. For many Customers, the convenience of Love Field's location near downtown Dallas made it a popular choice with business travelers, many of whom were willing to put up with the restrictions. At the same time, Southwest added flights from other Texas airports, such as Houston (Hobby) and El Paso, and originated more flights in cities such as Albuquerque, Phoenix, and Las Vegas, which were beyond the Wright restrictions.

The Company continued to grow despite the restrictions at Love Field, and after so many years of legal battles, it didn't want to reignite old hostilities. But the Wright Amendment wasn't good for the flying public. Without Southwest providing a low-fare option, air travelers paid a lot more for long-haul flights out of DFW than they should have.

In fact, it was that frustration that led to the first cracks in the Wright Amendment. In 1997, Senator Richard Shelby of Alabama, angered by high air fares in his state, argued that lifting the amendment would lower ticket prices for his constituents. His efforts led to the Shelby Amendment, which added Alabama, Kansas, and Mississippi to the permitted destinations from Love Field.

After years of declaring itself "passionately neutral" on the Wright Amendment, Southwest decided in 2004 that enough was enough. By then, DFW's annual air traffic was exceeding its capacity, and the Company stepped up its fight to repeal the restrictions. New CEO Gary Kelly publicly declared the Wright Amendment "outdated and outmoded," and Southwest launched a robust grassroots campaign, focused on an appeal to "Set Love Free." Congress finally listened and voted to reform the Wright Amendment in 2006, paving the way for Southwest, beginning in 2014, to fly nonstop anywhere within the United States from Love Field.

A Legendary Culture Takes Flight

Defining the Southwest Spirit

Southwest

From Hot Pants to Cool Colors

As it prepared to take to the skies in 1971, Southwest needed to attract attention—and Customers. Because of all the legal fights and the cost of acquiring planes and other equipment, the Company didn't have a lot of money left for marketing. It needed to create a personality for the airline that would set it apart from other carriers.

As the primary contact with Customers, Flight Attendants—or Hostesses as they were known at the time—were a main focus.

More than 1,200 women applied for the 40 original Hostess positions. The uniforms were a clear reflection of the times: bright red and orange hot pants, white lace-up go-go boots, and wide belts that hung on their hips. The Hostesses were featured prominently in the Company's advertising campaigns, and one, Sandra Force, even appeared on the cover of *Esquire* magazine in 1974.

Southwest's uniforms have gone from fun to functional to simply fabulous, and they've always been distinctive.

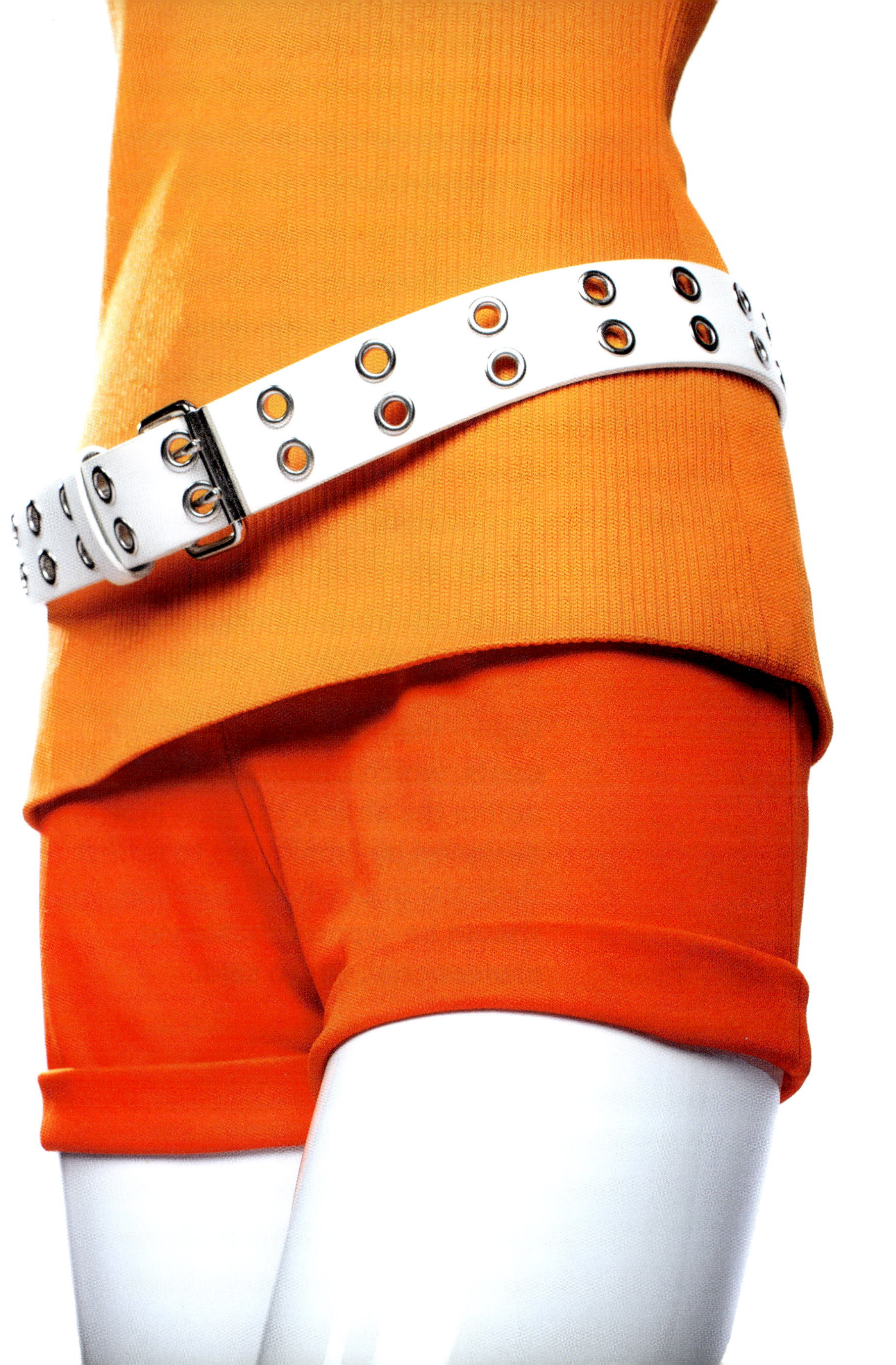

Three years after it began flying, Southwest launched a new line of uniforms: orange blouses with white polka dots and rusty orange aviator jackets. The hot pants, however, remained.

The uniforms were further refined in 1980, with earthy-brown suit jackets, cream blouses, and sleeveless V-necked sweaters. The hot pants were still a part of the uniform, but the boots were no longer lace-up, and they were brown instead of white.

The hot pants era officially ended by 1983, when Southwest introduced new uniforms for all Frontline Employees—pinstriped shirts, slacks or skirts, and blazers. The Company adopted similar uniforms for Ticket and Operations Agents. The designs were selected by a committee of Employees who worked in uniformed positions.

In 1986, to align with a marketing campaign called "Fun Fares," Southwest introduced "Fun Wear"—its first casual uniform that could be worn by Operations Employees on Fridays through Sundays and Office Staff on Fridays. The Fun Wear pieces included bright-colored jams and red shirts.

In 1990, Southwest adopted its Signal Uniforms, which incorporated navy blazers and tailored dresses and suits for Customer-facing Employees, and slacks, dress shirts, and "speedsuits" for those on the Ramp and in Provisioning or Maintenance. The uniforms incorporated tiny emblems based on maritime signal flags arranged to spell "S.W.A."

Six years later, the Company chose a new style that went in a more casual direction all year long—collared navy or white shirts with khaki shorts. The new line was wildly popular with Employees and set Southwest apart from other carriers. Vice President Inflight Operations Sonya Lacore, a former Flight Attendant who wore the khaki shorts, said they worked well for years, but the Company probably kept them too long.

In 2015, Southwest enlisted 43 Employees from across the Company to weigh in and help refine new uniform designs. After much debate—try getting such a diverse group to agree on fashion—they selected styles of charcoal and navy accented by the bright red, yellow, and blue of the airplane livery.

"We were trying to go for something a little more bold and modern," said Sonya, who oversaw the carrier's process.

Unlike the hot pants and go-go boots, which Leadership chose to define the airline, the new look was designed by Employees to reflect their vision of what the airline should be—approachable yet professional, Sonya said.

In keeping with Southwest's Core Values, which encourage Employees to be themselves at work, the new uniforms included 75 separate pieces that Employees can mix and match. Even Pilots got a new look, although it was subtle: They switched their suits from navy to black.

After almost 20 years of khaki shorts, the new, more stylish look is a big hit with Employees.

↑
Flight Attendants Alphonso Thomas, Tracye Tipps, and Joey Reynolds model the Employee-designed Heart uniforms in May 2016.

Unseating the Competition

It wasn't just Southwest's open-seating policy that was unusual; some of the seats themselves were configured in a way that was anything but ordinary.

One of the distinctive features of Southwest's early aircraft was the lounge seating—reversed seats around the over-wing exits and in the front and rear of some planes. The seats were a fixture in its aircraft for more than 30 years, and they were popular with many business flyers, who used them for "meetings in the sky." They were also popular with families traveling as a group. Other Customers found they were a way to meet new people or felt they contributed to the Fun-LUVing atmosphere for which the Company is famous. And while not all Customers loved them, they became a distinctive trademark.

When it launched the 737-700 in 1997, Southwest began to move away from the lounge seating because of new safety guidelines. In 2001, it switched to the Spirit livery and interior and gradually replaced lounge seating in many of its older airplanes when they came in for routine maintenance. In 2005, the Company retired its last 737-200, and with it, the last of the lounge seats.

Over the years, Southwest has continued to focus on seat design as a way of improving the Customer Experience. It's not as easy as it sounds. If seats are too heavy, it increases fuel consumption. But they also must be strong enough to accommodate Customers of all sizes and to withstand the force of an emergency impact. In 1983, the Company began adding seats with cool natural fibers trimmed with leather. The seats, which were wide and more comfortable, reflected the red and desert gold of the aircraft.

The Spirit livery and interior adopted in 2001 included Canyon Blue-and-tan leather seating throughout. In 2012, Southwest unveiled the EVOLVE interiors, an eco-friendly and cost-efficient new look. It also was able to increase seating to 143 from 137 per plane without sacrificing Customers' personal space. These interiors offered more under-seat space for carry-on bags, and the seats were made from scuff-resistant eLeather, which incorporated natural fibers into their design.

Each seat was lighter by six pounds, reducing the weight per plane by 635 pounds, generating fuel savings of about $10 million annually across the fleet.

The Heart cabin, introduced in 2016, has a seat design that brings Customers additional space and comfort with more leg room. The widest economy 737 seat, it features an adjustable headrest, enhanced back and bottom comfort, and more room to hold personal belongings. The seats are upholstered in Southwest's Bold Blue eLeather, used in the EVOLVE interiors.

While its competitors may try to pack more people into as small a space as possible to boost profits, Southwest continues to keep the focus on Customers, offering them a combination of comfort and utility that has been the Company's approach to seating since the days of the bulkhead lounges.

→ **Southwest introduced its Heart cabin in May 2016.**

↓ **Herb serves peanuts to Customers seated in lounge seats in October 1991.**

SOUTH
kickn

Armed and Humorous

For the epic Malice in Dallas event, Herb came prepared for battle, including all the "essentials."

On a barren stretch of Industrial Boulevard between downtown Dallas and the Trinity River, the Sportatorium was built in 1935 and gained fame as a wrestling and music venue. In March 1992, though, it hosted what was undoubtedly its most prestigious event—Malice in Dallas.

The showdown featured Southwest Airlines fan favorite "Smokin'" Herb Kelleher against the chairman of an aviation company in South Carolina, "Killer" Kurt Herwald, battling for the pride of the skies ... or at least the right to use the marketing slogan "Just Plane Smart."

The contenders spent weeks in rigorous training, with Killer Kurt pumping iron and Smokin' Herb curling fifths of his favorite whiskey and, at one point, walking up a flight of stairs.

Smokin' Herb arrived at the packed arena with a busload of cheerleaders, who also happened to be Southwest Flight Attendants. He was wearing a white robe and black boots, with a pack of cigarettes and mini bottles of whiskey taped to each one. His arm was in a sling because, he explained, he'd had to stop and save a child's life on Interstate 35 on the way to the match. As he stepped into the ring, the crowd went wild, and Smokin' Herb settled into the recliner strategically placed in his corner.

SOUTHWEST AIRLINES
20 YEARS OF LOVING YOU

At the bell, the two contenders came to the center of the ring, sat down at a table, and clasped hands. Smokin' Herb, cigarette dangling from his mouth, put up a few seconds of resistance before Killer Kurt slammed his hand onto the tabletop. Smokin' Herb crawled out of the ring and loaded himself onto a waiting stretcher.

Before Smokin' Herb was hauled away, though, Killer Kurt, gracious to the end, said he'd decided to let Southwest use the "Just Plane Smart" slogan anyway, and they both agreed to give a combined $15,000 to charity.

To this day, Malice in Dallas is cited in textbooks and by professors at the University of Pennsylvania's Wharton School of Business as an extreme bout of marketing brilliance. Some studies have suggested that Southwest gained $6 million worth of free publicity. And Kurt? He later said his aviation company, a fixed-based operator in Greenville, South Carolina, grew 25 percent a year for four years after the event.

(The event even caught the attention of the *NBC Nightly News with Tom Brokaw*, whose reporter felt a need to remind viewers that one of the wrestlers was "the CEO of a Fortune 500 company.")

The whole thing started after Southwest ran TV ads with the slogan "Just Plane Smart," which a marketing executive from the aviation company thought sounded a bit too close to their own slogan, "Plane Smart." He fired off a letter to Southwest suggesting that they settle the matter with a winner-take-all arm-wrestling contest. Kurt thought the letter was a lark, but Herb, always up for some old-fashioned hijinks, not only accepted the challenge but alerted the press to the upcoming showdown.

"This is going to be cool," Herb told Kurt. "We'll have a blast doing this."

The entire event was classic Herb, epitomizing one of his management tropes: "We take our competition seriously, but not ourselves."

←
"Smokin' Herb" grimaces during the Malice in Dallas showdown on March 20, 1992, a spectacle staged to settle a marketing dispute.

A Building for the People

Technically, Southwest's first headquarters was Founder Herb Kelleher's law office in San Antonio, which happened to be across the street from the St. Anthony Club, where the famous napkin session gave birth to the Company.

One of the first executive decisions Lamar Muse made after he was hired as President in 1971 was to confirm Dallas (Love Field) would be the airline's home, even though Herb and fellow Founder Rollin King lived in San Antonio.

"Where Rollin and Herb lived was of no consequence," Lamar said. "Since we were going to be flying initially from Dallas to Houston and from Dallas to San Antonio, and since most future service points in Texas would be primarily from Dallas, I determined that Company headquarters should be in Dallas, not San Antonio." As a result, Southwest set up shop in what had been, until the 1930s, the original passenger terminal at Love Field.

When Southwest broke ground on its Headquarters, Employees helped with the design, and the result was a vibrant space that embodies the Southwest Spirit.

Headquarters Building
Ground Breaking
November 15, 1988

↑
A three-dimensional depiction of the famous Malice in Dallas event inside Southwest's Headquarters building in 2010.

Three years later, in 1974, the Company moved to a low-rise office building at 1820 Regal Row, near Stemmons Freeway, and then moved back to Love Field in 1979. After most of the other airlines had moved to Dallas/Fort Worth Regional Airport, much of Love Field was unused, and Southwest took over the old Braniff Terminal on the North Concourse for its offices. As the airline continued to expand during the next decade, however, it outgrew the terminal space.

In 1987, planning began on the new headquarters, or General Offices ("GO") as they called it, at the current location on the west side of Love Field, off Denton Drive. Construction started in 1989, took 13 months to complete, and cost $15 million—less than the cost of a new 737. The 254,000-square-foot building included an outdoor deck on the third floor that offered a view of the Love Field runway, so Employees could see Company planes taking off and landing.

The Company added square footage to these General Offices three times before expanding the Corporate Campus in 2014 to include a new building, the Training and Operational Support (TOPS) building. The Leadership Education and Aircrew Development (LEAD) Center was added in 2017, and Wings, which houses offices and training facilities for Operational Departments, was added in 2018. In all, the Corporate Campus now encompasses more than a million square feet.

When the General Offices on Love Field Drive were being designed in the late 1980s, the Company relied on Employee suggestions on the building layout. Departments that worked together frequently were located strategically next to each other. Colleen, who was Vice President Administration at the time, banned department heads from the planning committee. Rank-and-file Employees, she reasoned, would focus more on function and efficiency than management perks such as office size.

"The Southwest Employees have had a direct role in many of the decisions for the new facility and are really excited about the move," then-Project Manager Robert Dorsey said at the time.

As for his own office, Herb gave the architect specific instructions—no windows. After all, if the CEO had no windows, Employees wouldn't jockey for an office with a better view. Besides, having no windows meant more wall space he could fill with pictures of his heroes, which included former presidents, an aviation pioneer, and a former British Prime Minister.

Just as Herb filled his office with mementos that held significance for him, the rest of the building became a showcase for Employees. Corridor walls became vertical museums constantly being updated with photographs of events. When the building opened, the walls were covered with some 2,000 items, from newspaper clippings, to letters from grateful mayors, to snapshots of Employee celebrations, to Employees' family and pet photos. The items were rotated over the years to different hallways and floors, so the views were constantly changing. Colleen once described it as "our scrapbook on the walls."

The Company designated areas for items too big to hang on the walls, setting up display cases for old Hostess uniforms, the Quicket Machine, and a custom motorcycle given to Herb by Pilots at one of the annual chili cookoffs. There's even a corporate time capsule with mementos donated by Employees—and a half-finished bottle of whiskey from Herb. By 2005, the number of items on the walls and in the display areas topped 18,000.

These "wall-seums" also served as a training guide and reference library. Interns and New Hires were often sent on scavenger hunts, scouring the walls to answer questions about Company history.

When a member of the Communications Team needed to verify a date or other detail, then-Senior Vice President Culture & Communications Ginger Hardage might tell them to "go to the wall."

Starting in 2012, the Company refined the wall displays into Culture Centers, special zones throughout the building for collaboration and social gathering, each with a unique theme, including Company memorabilia, milestones, and other celebrations of the Core Values. One Culture Center even has a button that, when pushed, plays recordings of Herb's distinctive laughs. Company conference rooms are assigned themes that reflect key aspects of the Culture.

The Corporate Campus has always been a home not just for the Employees who work there, but for all Southwest Employees, regardless of where they're based. As the Company has grown, it has exported a little bit of Headquarters to other work locations, which now have their own Culture Walls.

In another tribute to its People, Southwest put the name of each of its 60,000 Employees at the time on the windows of the pedestrian bridge that spans Denton Drive connecting the Headquarters building on the current-day Corporate Campus, TOPS, and Wings.

After Herb's passing in 2019, Colleen gave Southwest the most poignant cultural touchstone of all—statues of the famous Founder in an iconic pose about to throw a paper airplane. They stand in glass cases, prominently displayed in the lobbies of multiple buildings on Campus. (Herb's office, by the way, was preserved, itself a time capsule of sorts.)

In 2021, Headquarters was renamed in Herb's honor. It's a fitting remembrance for the man who changed the history of commercial aviation and a building designed by and for the People he inspired the most.

From Chalkboards to Starships

In the early days, Southwest approached everything with an eye toward frugality and simple, manual processes. The original Reservations Department was just a room with folding tables with phones on them. Reservations were recorded on index cards.

Over the years, the airline has evolved from handwritten flight-tracking records to managing flights in real time from a high-tech control center.

Next to Reservations was Dispatch, which had a single teleprinter machine—for weather updates—and a phone. In the center of the room was a large counter with an aerial map, and similar maps hung on the wall. The latest weather updates were attached to a clipboard and set out on the counter for Pilots to review before their flights, along with other notices such as runway construction or equipment outages.

"The Pilot would go in and get a weather briefing from the Dispatcher there in Dallas face-to-face," said Vice President Flight Operations Bob Waltz, who joined Southwest as a First Officer in 2000. "They'd get their information handed to them, and then off they flew."

Flights were tracked on a chalkboard on the wall of the Operations Office, and most forms were filled out in pencil. Calculations were done largely by hand.

BNA 214 MDW
0925 1040
MDW 894 CLE
1115 1215
CLE 894 BWI
1235 1340
BWI 1316 CLE
1400 1505
CLE 1316 MDW
1530 1635
MDW 219 MCI
1800 1915
MCI 219 TUL
1935 2025
BWI 861 SDF
1010 1135
SDF 861 STL
1155 1300
STL 547 BWI
1320 1530
PSD947/CMH/:50
BWI 359 BHM
1555 1745
BHM 359 MSY
1815 1920
BWI 1280 CLE
1015 1120
CLE 1280 MDW
1140 1245
MDW 549 MCI
1305 1420
MCI 549 TUL
1440 1530

In March 1973, the Company expanded and moved 17 Agents into the Dallas Reservations Center. They had their own chalkboard that displayed flights and fare information. As reservations came in, they would cross seats off the board.

As Southwest's network expanded, so did all of these operations. Ticker tape-style machines were replaced by faster, quieter terminals that resembled desktop computers. Reservations were stored in a Bunker-Ramo mainframe, and entries consisted of flights, the number of seats, and the names of Customers. The system allowed Ticket Agents to confirm reservations, although the tickets themselves were still sold through the "Love Machine" cash registers.

As late as 1999, First Officers would jot down their flight times on a beverage napkin and hand it to the Operations Agent working the flight. The Ops Agent would then enter the data into the Dispatch Report Builder before throwing the napkin away. Southwest replaced the napkin-based system with the Operations Terminal Information System, or OTIS, which allowed First Officers to review and approve flight times from reports handed to them by the Ops Agent when they arrived at the gate. The flight data was shared in real time with Ground Ops, Flight Ops, Tech Ops, Inflight, and other departments.

In 2000, the Company deployed its Southwest Integrated Flight Tracking System, or SWIFT, which provided flight management capabilities in real time. SWIFT allowed Data Managers to get status reports on flight tracking, fuel usage, Customer loads, Crew management, gate information, and weather reports.

In 2015, as part of a sweeping, multiyear $800 million technological transformation, Southwest created "The Baker," a tool that improves ontime performance on days when things such as bad weather disrupt the network. "The Baker" was developed by Southwest Dispatchers, including Mike Baker. The program is named in Mike's honor and continues to help Southwest anticipate potential delays and reroute aircraft. In its first year, it boosted Southwest's ontime performance by 10 to 15 percent on days with irregular operations, and its overall ontime performance by 2 percent.

All of this new technology, combined with a growing number of destinations, flights, and Employees, made the face-to-face coordination of flights from the early days impossible. By 2020, Southwest served more than 100 airports, and before the 2020 COVID-19 pandemic, was operating more than 4,000 flights a day that carried nearly half a million Customers in peak travel seasons. Coordinating all those flights required a more complex mechanism, which became the Network Operations Control (NOC). With its giant flat-panel screens and banks of computers tracking real-time data, it's about as far removed from the old chalkboards and weather printouts as a tricycle from an F-16.

"It went from small offices, a lot of telephone work, limited automation to what looks like you're on the bridge of an intergalactic spaceship today," said Bob, who helped set up the modern-day NOC and later became the first Pilot to serve as Network Director.

"It's the nerve center of the operation. That's where all the Teams come together." Operations such as Maintenance, Dispatch, Flight Crew Scheduling, Meteorology, Safety & Security, and Network Customer Specialists all coordinate daily operations through the NOC.

"That area tells the maturation of Southwest Airlines from a small carrier into a major player" with international operations, including the Extended Operations (ETOPS) authorization for flights to Hawaii, Bob said. "All of those things require a certain level of operational control and coordination that is so important, and that we wouldn't have been able to do without the NOC."

Through their dedication, hard work, and innovative thinking, the People of Southwest have brought things a long way from the days of index cards and beverage napkins.

In May 2014, Southwest opened its state-of-the-art Network Operations Control center in Dallas.

SAT
SAM
ANTONIO
HOU
HOUSTON
SOUTHWEST AIRLINES
DAL
DALLAS
22-71-36
22-71-36
DALLAS
SOUTHWEST AIRLINES

Ramping Up

Loading bags and provisioning planes may have looked different in 1971, but the same Southwest Spirit remains.

The 10-Minute Turn became possible because of Employees like Larry Dzieranowski. Larry joined Southwest in San Antonio in 1975 after he was discharged from the Marine Corps.

Of course, when Larry started, things were a little less formal than they are now. A relative had told him about a new airline, and he thought it might need workers. He walked into Southwest's office in the San Antonio airport and asked the Station Manager at the time, Dennis Lardon, if the Company was taking applications.

"He said, 'We don't have any applications. Just give me your name, and put it on a piece of paper here, and I'll give you a ring,'" Larry recalled. He wondered what kind of operation he'd stumbled into, but a few days later Dennis called him and, after an interview, offered him a job as a Ramp Agent. "I had no clue what I was walking into," Larry said.

Training was also less formal. "They would say, 'This is the tug. This is how you start it and go to the airplane.' It was just that kind of deal." San Antonio had about seven Ramp Agents, and they did everything.

Typically, three People worked the plane. One marshalled the aircraft to the gate, using their hands to guide the Captain (Southwest didn't have lighted wands at the time). Then the other two Employees would begin unloading bags, starting with the front compartment and then moving to the back.

The Employee who had guided the aircraft to the gate would usually also position the jet bridge to allow Customers to deplane. Then they would run down to the transfer, or "T-Point," where the bags for the outbound flight were coming down the conveyor from the ticket counter. They would load the bags on the cart and pull it around to the forward compartment. They would take the bags that had come off the plane back to the T-Point while the other two Employees loaded the bags for the next flight, starting with the forward compartment, then moving to the rear.

"We used to have contests to see if we could bury the guy in the bin, throwing the bags on the belt real fast," recalled retired Vice President Airport Affairs Bob Montgomery, who started as a part-time Ramp Agent in Lubbock in 1977. "They'd stack up until you'd win, [which was] when he had to turn off the belt loader because they were jamming up inside, and then you'd make fun of each other."

Meanwhile, the third worker would typically fill the ice bins in the galley, then prepare to pull the jet bridge back as the plane departed.

"I don't know how we did it," Larry said, laughing.

It helped that Southwest had only four destinations at the time, and baggage tags were color-coded. "Red goes to Dallas; green goes to Harlingen," Larry said. "You can't screw that up."

Long before baggage tags were scanned, Ramp Agents provided the Captain with an estimated bag count. Today, every bag must be meticulously accounted for. Before 9/11, baggage systems typically had one belt that collected the bags and took them to the transfer point. Today, all bags must first go through centralized screening machines operated by the Transportation Security Administration, and the systems are far more complex.

Those changes mean it takes longer to get bags loaded on the plane, but Ramp Agents still work to turn planes efficiently, and the Company has scaled its processes and implemented new technology to adapt to the increased operational complexity. The shared commitment to getting the plane loaded accurately and pushed back safely remains the ultimate Team sport at Southwest. When Larry started, times were much different, but the Southwest Spirit was still the same.

He described the job as one that required strength, endurance, and a dash of ingenuity.

If the ice machine was broken, an Employee would run to a nearby motel and raid its ice machines so they could restock the planes. Southwest didn't have its own glycol machines for de-icing back then, so Ramp Agents had to borrow one from other carriers.

The Spirit and camaraderie of those earlier years made work fun, and Larry rarely missed a day. In the early 1980s, Southwest gave a microwave oven to Employees who hadn't missed a shift during the year. Nearly four decades later, Larry still had his. "That sucker still works," he said in the fall of 2020.

Sadly, Larry passed away in early 2021. He might not have known what he was walking into back in 1975, but it didn't take him long to realize he'd found something special. He stayed with the Company for almost 46 years, and Southwest was proud to have him on the frontlines all that time.

↑
A Ramp Agent guides a Southwest flight to the gate in Salt Lake City in 2019.

←
Ramp Agents load bags onto a flight in Salt Lake City in 2019.

That's the Ticket

Southwest's original idea for selling tickets was simple—keep all fares the same and as low as possible, and don't assign seats. All it needed was cash registers, which it called "Love Machines," and credit card imprinters, and it could issue a ticket in less than 10 seconds. Customers took the receipt to the gate and exchanged it for a boarding pass.

Of course, most Customers were used to the multilayered, carbon-copy tickets that major airlines issued, so many would lose the cash register receipts or throw them away. Southwest's Executives stewed over the problem. Should they follow industry tradition and print actual tickets? Former Executive Vice President and Chief Operations Officer Gary Barron had a better idea. "Why don't we just print 'THIS IS A TICKET' in big, bold red letters on the receipt?" Gary's inspired solution saved the Company about $2 million on ticket printers, and it continued to use receipts as tickets until 1989.

It might have looked like something out of a 1950s science fiction movie, but the Quicket Machine was just one of many Southwest ticketing innovations.

QUICKET
1 Use Credit Card as shown
2 Press Destination Button
3 Press Appropriate Fare Class Button
4 Press One-Way or Roundtrip
5 Wait for Ticket Go to Boarding Gate
3 SELECT FARE
PEAK
OFF PEAK
PEAK/ OFF PEAK
NIGHT FARE
SPECIAL #1
ALBUQUERQUE
AUSTIN
BIRMINGHAM
CHICAGO (MIDWAY)
CORPUS CHRISTI
DETROIT CITY
DETROIT METRO
EL PASO
HARLINGEN
HOUSTON HOBBY (SOUTH)
INDIANAPOLIS
KANSAS CITY (INTERNATIONAL)
LAS VEGAS
LITTLE ROCK
MIDLAND/ ODESSA
NASHVILLE
NEW ORLEANS
OAKLAND
OKLAHOMA CITY
ONTARIO
PHOENIX
RENO
ST. LOUIS
SAN ANTONIO
SAN DIEGO
SAN FRANCISCO
TULSA
4 SELECT TRIP
ONE WAY
ROUND TRIP
CANCEL
2 SELECT DESTN
DISCOUNT FARES NOT AVAILABLE THROUGH THIS MACHINE. PLEASE SEE AGENT. THANK YOU.
• USE CREDIT CARD WITH MAGNETIC STRIPE
• POSITION CARD AS SHOWN
• USING DOWN PRESSURE QUICKLY SLIDE CARD THROUGH THE LENGTH OF THE SLOT
1 INSERT CREDIT CARD
1A INSERT PIN
CLR
ENT

Back then, Southwest sold most tickets straight from the ticket counter, but a few years after it started flying, a terminal renovation at Love Field curtailed parking at the airport. The Company didn't have offices in downtown areas or major hotels like some of its larger competitors, so the lack of parking threatened its sales. The solution: The Company opened a drive-through ticket office at the corner of Mockingbird Lane and Cedar Springs Road in Dallas, near the airport entrance. Customers could grab a ticket without leaving their cars—a major convenience at the time.

Southwest's simple ticketing system, however, may have been too simple. Some Customers couldn't believe the Company wasn't offering discounts for advance purchases. At a Dallas cocktail party, a business executive approached Herb and said he'd noticed that American Airlines was offering fares as low as Southwest's. The difference, Herb explained, was that passengers had to buy a ticket on American 30 days in advance to get that fare. On Southwest, Customers could walk up, pay the same price, and get right on the plane. The man refused to believe that Southwest's low fares came with no strings attached.

Eventually, the Company decided to offer advance-purchase discounts as well, which introduced it to yield management, a variable pricing strategy that enabled Southwest to maximize the number of Customers per flight. As a result, the Company learned to sell more seats at even lower fares. But a more complicated fare structure also meant it needed a more advanced sales process. Several Employees, sitting in a bar in the late 1970s, came up with the solution: create a ticket machine that worked like an ATM. In 1979, Southwest introduced Automated Ticket Vending Machines, or ATVMs, known affectionately as the "Quicket Machine." (In advertising, the process was referred to as a "QuickieTicket.")

↑
Herb demonstrates the ease of buying a ticket from an automated Quicket Machine at the Dallas (Love Field) Ticket Counter in 1985.

It was a console that looked a little like a computer from a 1950s science fiction movie. Customers swiped a credit card, punched a button for their destination, chose one-way or round trip, and Quicket printed their ticket. Of course, Southwest's route system was expanding, and it soon ran out of buttons. Rather than have the manufacturer retrofit the machines at great expense, then-Director Technical Services Mike Golden put together an internal Team and upgraded the machines, which saved about $1 million.

By the 1990s, airlines had developed more advanced computer reservation systems. At first, most of the systems, which were owned by some of Southwest's biggest competitors, listed its flights without charging for the service. It was a direct link to travel agents, who accounted for 35 to 40 percent of Southwest's business at the time. When the owners of the reservation systems tried to raise their fees, Southwest refused to pay, and the other airlines kicked the Company off their systems. "It was intended to be a dagger in the heart and cut off a lot of the sales flow to Southwest," said Chairman and CEO Gary Kelly, who was Vice President Finance & Chief Financial Officer at the time. Agents had to call the Company's reservations desk and book tickets over the phone—a major inconvenience.

Again, Southwest came up with a work-around for its competitors' roadblocks.

In January 1995, it developed the first completely Ticketless Travel system, known as Southwest Airlines Travel, or SWAT.

The SWAT system allowed travel agents to log directly into the Company's reservation system, the first true e-ticketing in the industry.

In March 1995, with the advent of the World Wide Web, Southwest took the ticketless concept a step further. It launched the "Home Gate" portal as part of its website—the industry's first—iflyswa.com. Three months later, it linked to TravelWeb, which opened the door for Customers to book their own airline travel on the "Home Gate" that next year.

Between SWAT and the launch of the website, Southwest had declared its independence from the computer reservation systems (CRSs) of others. "That was really the dagger in the heart of the CRSs, and it worked obviously to our great favor," Gary said.

Security measures added after 9/11 required more changes to Southwest's system, and it traded in its famous reusable plastic boarding passes for paper ones printed with each Customer's information. The first automated pass was issued at Houston Intercontinental Airport in 2002, and a year later, Southwest began testing bar code readers at gates to speed boarding even more. In 2004, it added the capability for Customers to print them at home.

A decade later, in 2014, Southwest's ticketing process took another technological leap forward, when it began offering mobile boarding passes on Customers' smartphones. Today, about half of the Company's ticket sales come via mobile phones, and more than 90 percent of its Customers use their phones to check in for flights and get an electronic boarding pass. It's almost like having a Love Machine at your fingertips.

↓
In 2014, Southwest rolled out mobile boarding passes, which make getting through the airport quicker and greener.

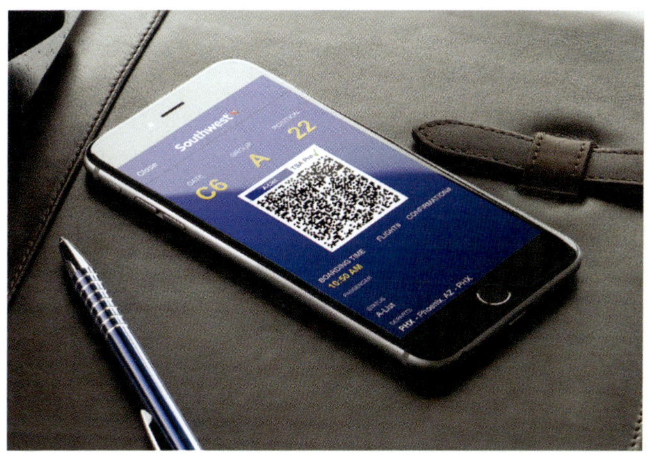

Values of the Heart

Southwest's Values are at the Heart of everything the Company believes in.

It all started with chili. Sure, Southwest pays tribute to its unique Values, rooted in Herb's legal crusading, which helped get the Company off the ground. And, of course, it honors Colleen's motherly touch. She more than anyone defined and refined the Culture over the years. But don't underestimate the importance of the chili.

By 1973, after constant legal battles and repeated challenges by competitors, including Braniff's attempt to crush Southwest with the $13 fare war, Employees were accustomed to predictions of the Company's doom. Almost every morning, it seemed, Texas newspapers were publishing discouraging stories about Southwest's survival prospects. Clearly, there was only one thing to do: throw a party.

Rich Robertson, who worked in Marketing, decided to throw the "First and Last Chili Cookoff," a tongue-in-cheek recognition that the Company might not survive long enough to have a second one. The cookoff—or more specifically, the attitude behind it—became a rallying point for Employees. It galvanized the Southwest Spirit and formed the foundation of Southwest's Fun-LUVing Culture. (Far from being the last, by 2020, when the cookoff was virtual because of the COVID-19 pandemic, the Company had hosted the cookoff for 47 consecutive years. By then, the annual event was one of the longest-running chili festivals in the world.)

Certainly, the legal fights in the early days helped lay the foundation for Southwest's Culture. "The warrior mentality, the very fight to survive, is truly what created our Culture," Colleen said.

But it was more than just a survival instinct. Herb knew that simply flying planes wasn't enough. The Company needed a purpose, and that purpose was serving Customers.

Many of Southwest's Original Employees had either been fired or laid off by other carriers. "Because they had been burned so badly, they were willing to do things they would never have done at the places they worked before, because [at Southwest] they were being treated with respect," Colleen noted.

Those two qualities—respect and the fight for survival—forged the basis of Southwest Culture.

After Colleen joined the Company as Corporate Secretary in 1978, Herb put her in charge of the People Department (then called Personnel) and Customers, and the Culture began to take shape. She reinforced the message that Customer Service was paramount. She instilled The Golden Rule at the core of Southwest's Values. Her mother had taught her empathy and that "you should treasure honesty and pride in who you are as a human being."

Colleen also established a sense of priority that's unusual in many companies—Employees come first. Herb and Colleen believed that Employees could serve Customers only if they had loving support from Leaders and Coworkers and they were confident in that support. In other words, they needed to know their bosses had their backs.

That meant acknowledging that the Customer is *not* always right. Sometimes, Customers can be abusive or make unreasonable demands. Herb famously told a complaining Customer who threatened to take her business elsewhere, "We will miss you."

As the Company grew in both size and the number of communities it served, reinforcing the Culture across an increasingly disparate workforce became more challenging.

In 1990, Colleen formed what became known as the Companywide Culture Committee. "The reason we started the first Culture Committee was that we were really starting to spread out in our system, and because of the Wright Amendment, we could not get the Employees from, say, California into Dallas unless they had three days off," she said. "I had always been able to have People see and feel and touch the Culture that existed in our Headquarters, but now we couldn't. That's why I started the Culture Committee, because if we couldn't bring Employees to the Culture, we needed some kind of group that could bring the Culture to them."

The Committee started with 48 Employees from around the Company who exemplified the Southwest Spirit. As of 2021, it had about 400 Culture Ambassadors, with volunteer Members dedicated to empowering Employees to own, strengthen, and promote Southwest's Culture.

Over the years, the Company's Core Values have evolved, but they are still based on a two-way commitment between Southwest and its Employees. The Company promises to provide a stable work environment and equal opportunity for personal growth. Employees are given the same concern, respect, and caring attitude within the Company that the Company expects them to give to Customers.

In exchange, Employees promise to live the Southwest Way: demonstrate a Warrior Spirit—work hard, strive to be the best, and be courageous; lead with a Servant's Heart—put others first and live by The Golden Rule; and display a Fun-LUVing Attitude—be a passionate Team Player, have fun, and don't take yourself too seriously.

These shared commitments are built around nine simple Values, divided into three categories: "Me," "We," and "Southwest."

"Me" refers to the personal attitude and behavior Employees show at work every day: Pride, Integrity, and Humility. "We" is about Teamwork, Honesty, and "Service with LUV"—how Employees treat others. "Southwest," of course, means how everyone works together to help the Company succeed. These qualities include Efficiency, Discipline, and Excellence.

The evolution of Southwest's Culture and Core Values is remarkable because the Company has been able to maintain a loving environment in an industry known for fierce competition.

"You can fight hard, you can be a tough competitor, you can get it done, you can win, and you can even dominate a market, but you never lose sight of your Core Values," Vice Chairman Ron Ricks said. "You never lose sight of [the fact that] that this tough fighting is a means to an end, and the end is to accomplish something that's really good."

↓
First Officer Michael Boos boards *Heart One* in August 2014, shortly after seeing for the first time the bold new look that captures Southwest's Heart and Core Values.

'Hire Me!'

Not every company would ask job applicants to change pants during an interview. But then, not every company has the unique hiring criteria of Southwest Airlines.

When considering whether to offer someone a job, Southwest's People Department looks for a particular attitude that indicates latent signs of the Southwest Spirit.

That's what the change of pants was all about. Many years ago, a group of eight Pilot applicants showed up for their interviews in typical attire—dark suits, black shoes, dress socks. The Recruiters asked if they would change into Bermuda shorts—they could keep their suit coats and dress shoes on—and spend the rest of the day interviewing in the mismatched outfits. Six of the eight were game, and they were hired.

"We do think it's very important to always show a healthy sense of humor," according to Colleen. "We've always told New Hires the same thing for years—we want them to take our business seriously, but we don't want them to take themselves too seriously."

At Southwest's orientation class, New Hires get a taste of the Company's encouragement to not take themselves too seriously.

ONBOARD
and living the Southwest way

Just as it had more than 1,200 women apply for its original 40 Hostess positions back in 1971, the Company has routinely had far more applicants than jobs. As the Southwest Culture gained national attention, and the Company was repeatedly recognized as a top place to work by different organizations, the flood of applications grew. Southwest typically hires less than 2 percent of applicants. In 2019, the Company received 356,000 applications and hired about 5,200.

Over the years, applicants hoping to beat the odds have tried to show off their Fun-LUVing Attitude and their do-whatever-it-takes mentality in their applications. People Department Director Lindsey Lang, who worked in several Southwest recruiting positions between 2001 and 2012, recalled one applicant who sent a cake featuring a picture of his child saying, "Hire my Daddy," and another who made a Southwest 737 out of toy blocks with a resume inside. Another resume came in the form of a sock puppet. Lindsey remembers one eager applicant standing outside Headquarters in a honey-loving bear costume holding a sign that said, "Hire Me."

Others' applications have come via singing telegram, accompanied by a dozen doughnuts, or posted on a billboard on Denton Drive near Company Headquarters. One applicant even paid for a tow plane to fly a "Hire Me" banner over Headquarters. (Unfortunately for that applicant, Southwest's offices don't have very big windows.)

Director Talent Acquisition Greg Muccio, who joined Southwest as a Lead Recruiter in 2001, recalls several instances of applicants sending him footwear in hopes of "getting their foot in the door."

It's the interview process, however, that makes the difference, because that's where Recruiters assess the attitudes of applicants and determine whether they fit with Southwest's Culture and Core Values.

↑
Herb and Colleen speak to attendees of Southwest's Summer Camp, which encourages high school students to consider careers with the Company.

"We target questions and foster an environment in the interview process to identify the right fit for folks that demonstrate our Southwest Values," Lindsey said.

The attitude and cultural fit are nonnegotiable. "It trumps experience," Greg said. "Recruiters can share candidates that may not have all the experiences we want, but they cannot submit someone where the Culture or Values fit is questionable."

↑
Southwest Employees are hired because they demonstrate the Company's Values and its Fun-LUVing Attitude.

Before the COVID-19 crisis, Southwest's voluntary turnover rate had historically been about 3 percent, while the transportation industry average typically ran several times higher.

Other companies, impressed by Southwest's low turnover, often study the Company in hopes of finding a "silver bullet" that's key to its hiring success. They often find it hard to believe that the driving principle of Southwest's process is simple: a dedication to its Culture.

"There is nothing unique about our process per se," said Shari Conaway, Senior Director Total Rewards in the People Department. "We just hire really tough and hire to the Southwest Values."

That means looking for individuals who care about others, not just themselves, who want to be a part of a Team, who understand the focus, and who genuinely want to help everyone on the Team succeed.

As Ellen Torbert, who retired in 2021 from her role as Vice President Diversity, Equity, & Inclusion, summarized it, "We foster a Culture that embraces and utilizes our diversity, as we value and celebrate our Employees in ways that are meaningful to them. That Servant's Heart—that is the key."

Well, that and a willingness to change pants.

Kicking Tail, Taking Names, and Showing Gratitude

Southwest has always believed that the best way to show Employees they're valued is to show that the Company cares about them. Celebrating successes isn't limited to work anniversaries or promotions; it's also about cheering events in their personal lives—birthdays, weddings, births, and "catching them doing good" at work.

"We celebrate little things, big things—we celebrate everything!" Colleen said. "Although we do have some formal celebrations, a lot of them are informal, spontaneous celebrations that cost little or no money."

While holidays such as Halloween tend to get the most media attention, inside the Company other celebrations often are even more significant. On Valentine's Day, the Company honors "Heroes of the Heart," for which Teams or Departments who work behind the scenes are nominated for recognition. The Company celebrates and recognizes the recipients, and their Team name is displayed for one year on the nose of an aircraft bearing the "Heroes of the Heart" insignia.

Balloons have often been a part of Southwest celebrations. The Company looks for fun ways to celebrate Employee successes.

↑ Members of the Companywide Culture Committee gathered in 2010 to recognize New Cohearts with Kick Tails.

Southwest's love of celebrations grew as the Company did. In the early days, it had one Christmas party, but as Southwest grew, it had to throw three. Colleen found it a bit overwhelming to coordinate three parties in the same month, so she started holding parties at other times of the year—Christmas in July in Oakland and in September in Chicago, for example. The anytime-is-Christmas parties were so popular that the Company started doing more of them at random times. They evolved into Spirit Parties and then eventually became known as Southwest Parties.

Just because companies get big doesn't mean they have to lose their entrepreneurial spirit or allow bureaucracy to override the decision-making of their employees. No matter how many employees you have, success comes from making them happy and proud of what they're doing. Southwest emphasizes the value of its Employees not just as workers—but as People.

After Gary Kelly became CEO in 2004, he wanted a way to quickly recognize Employees who were nominated by Coworkers for demonstrating Warrior Spirit, Servant's Heart, or Fun-LUVing Attitude. Retired Senior Director Employee Engagement Tonda Ferguson developed stickers for each of those categories that Employees could use to enter drawings for prizes. That became the Kick Tail™ program, through which Employees hand out personalized messages of thanks and encouragement to each other. The program then transitioned to the use of business card paper Kick Tails that Employees could use to recognize their Peers. In 2013, it partnered with a third-party vendor to develop a web-based platform to make it easier to track who was giving and receiving recognition.

Within the platform, known as SWAG (for "Southwest Airlines Gratitude"), Employees and Leaders are able to send and receive recognition to those who go above and beyond their daily responsibilities. This recognition comes in the form of SWAG Points and electronic Kick Tails (e-cards). The cards are themed to reflect the behavior for which the Employee is being recognized, including Teamwork, Living & Working the Southwest Way, Hospitality, and more.

When Employees receive Kick Tails, they're recorded in a database, and the Employees are entered in monthly drawings for SWAG Points and cash prizes.

SWAG Points never expire, and Employees can redeem them in a Rewards Mall for merchandise, gift cards, or travel on Southwest. "We have this common currency," Tonda said.

"If we gave everyone a key chain, not everybody would appreciate that, but if you give them the small amount of SWAG Points, their bank can continue to grow, and then they can get what they want."

In addition to the individual awards, Gary outlines a "Battle Plan" in an annual letter to Employees and sets goals for the Company to "Kick Tail" with their performance. For each goal met at the end of the year, every Employee gets a certain number of SWAG Points. In 2020, the COVID-19 pandemic undermined Gary's Battle Plan, and the Company suspended Kick Tail drawings as part of a larger plan to manage costs. Nevertheless, Employees continued to send Kick Tails to appreciate each other, and Leaders continued to recognize extraordinary efforts. A new Heart Strong e-card was also introduced to match the gravity of the 2020 moment, and in the three months following its introduction in late April, Employees sent almost 50,000 Kick Tails using the e-card.

As part of its 50th anniversary celebration, Southwest introduced the Kindness Kick Tail. The new Kick Tail encourages Employees to participate, alongside Customers and Partners, in a Company Challenge toward 1 Million Acts of Kindness in 2021.

Southwest is always looking for new reasons to celebrate, and this book you're reading is just one of them.

Rolled out in 2021, the Kindness Kick Tail allows Employees to recognize each other in celebration of Southwest's 1 Million Acts of Kindness Challenge during its 50th anniversary year.

Care in Action

Southwest's Internal Customer Care Team is there to celebrate and support Employees, whether it's with a T.J. LUV piggy bank or a shoulder to cry on.

In 2014, *Fortune* magazine set out to find "the coolest corporate gigs around." The magazine staffers looked for jobs that were unique to each company, and not surprisingly, they chose Southwest's Internal Customer Care (ICC) Team.

In the early days, Colleen Barrett, who began as Founder Herb Kelleher's secretary at his San Antonio law firm and later became Southwest's President, personally handled celebrating birthdays and anniversaries, sending sympathy cards, and offering support for other Employee life events or hardships.

"What Colleen really started was sharing love with our Employees when they were celebrating something wonderful or when they were going through a really hard time," said Managing Director Executive Office Nan Barry. "The Employee could have had a baby, gotten married, had a very serious illness, lost a parent, lost a spouse, had somebody graduating—it was really all-encompassing. What Colleen and Herb were doing informally was reaching out to these Employees with phone calls, with cards, with letters, and with gifts."

As Southwest grew, the ICC Team was formally established in the early 2000s to take over those duties on a larger scale. In 2019, the Company's four-person Team sent out 5,500 bereavement letters and more than 30,000 cards and gifts recognizing marriages, births, illnesses, and injuries. ICC's motto: If it matters to an Employee, it matters to us.

"It's just like family," Nan said. "The Company is right there with you when you're going through something really hard, and it just creates a loyalty that I can't even explain. You just feel such deep passion for the Company."

As just one example, in the early 2000s, an Employee was scheduled for an organ transplant close to Thanksgiving. The ICC Team tracked down the hotel where she was staying and had a holiday turkey and all the trimmings delivered.

Even the ICC Team, however, isn't immune from Southwest's overriding need to keep costs low. In 2020, facing one of the great challenges in its history—the COVID-19 pandemic—the Company relied on phone calls in lieu of sending cards and gifts by mail, and Employees expressed how much the gesture meant in a time of crisis. Even during the pandemic, when many Employees were working remotely, the ICC Team's love and care remained as strong as ever.

"Sometimes you get on the phone with someone, and they truly need to talk, and you are that person for them," said Executive Office Manager Andrea Mathews, who currently leads the ICC Team.

Working on the ICC Team can be emotionally taxing but also incredibly rewarding. ICC Members put their hearts into their jobs, Andrea said. The job description is definitely unusual: Team Members love others deeply and unselfishly open their hearts to everyone they can. Sometimes that means celebrating together. Other times, it means grieving together. If it matters to an Employee enough to let the ICC Team know, Southwest acknowledges it. From Employees buying their first home to being granted U.S. citizenship, the ICC Team's mission is always to celebrate the moments in the lives of others. It only takes a short amount of time to make a lasting impact by simply acknowledging important milestones. That is what a family does.

"It's a Company of almost 60,000 Employees," Nan said. "I tell people it's like a city. And everything happens in a city."

An Employee who was fighting cancer was disappointed when she couldn't attend the celebration for her 10-year anniversary with the Company because she wasn't feeling well. When the ICC Team found out, Team Members sent her a floral arrangement with Southwest flair: a dozen yellow roses in a blue vase with a red ribbon, delivered the same day as the gala.

When the daughter of an Employee lost her eyesight and had to learn Braille, an ICC Team Member who frequently works with children sent her gifts and toys that didn't require sight to enjoy. She also sent the child a card with a message written in Braille using fingernail polish. The child was delighted, as was the Employee.

The ICC Team regularly stays in touch with Employees who are battling life-threatening illnesses to reassure them that they are not alone in their fight. One Employee was called frequently but didn't respond to the voicemails the ICC Team left for him. They decided to pay him an in-person

↑
The Internal Customer Care (ICC) Team Members were honored as the 2007 Heroes of the Heart recipients, a prestigious distinction Colleen created to recognize behind-the-scenes work groups.

visit to make sure he was OK. He showed them that he had saved every voicemail. He said that on nights when he couldn't sleep or was having a hard time, he would play the voicemails, and they helped him find the strength to go on.

Of course, the ICC Team celebrates happy moments, too, such as sending a crystal vase when Employees get married or a congratulatory message from Chairman and CEO Gary Kelly for promotions. When Employees welcome a child or grandchild into the family, the ICC Team sends piggy banks shaped like a cartoon version of a Southwest plane to the parents and cards to the grandparents. Children's graduations also are celebrated, with new graduates receiving gifts such as headphones with the Southwest logo.

Whether it's a congratulations or a show of support during difficult times, the ICC Team can make a big impact on Employees' lives. Andrea not only helps to support Employees as a member of the Team, she has firsthand experience as a recipient as well. After her uncle was killed in a car accident, an ICC Team Member made sure her responsibilities were covered and that she could get home to her family. They also called the airport where she was arriving and had another Employee meet her plane to handle her luggage.

"They truly took care of every single piece of it," she recalled. "They put care into action."

Un-boo-lievable Fun

Halloween is one of the Company's favorite holidays, and like everything else at Southwest, there's a method to the madness.

Dressing up has always been part of Halloween at Southwest, but Chairman and CEO Gary Kelly embraces the holiday with gusto, participating in the sort of transformation you might expect to see on a movie set.

Months of planning go into each costume, which typically requires extensive makeup, wigs, and even prosthetics. Gary has been a loveable toy cowboy, a famous swashbuckling pirate, a long-bearded front man for a native Texas band, a kooky children's book character with an oversize green top hat and special yellow contact lenses, and even a fairy tale princess.

Employees pitch costume ideas throughout the year. In 2004, his first Halloween after becoming CEO, Gary went all out, dressing up as a famous front man for an American rock band known for face paint and pyrotechnics. In the years since, he portrayed a Kansas farm girl (he even toted a stuffed terrier in a Southwest-branded pet carrier) and a 1960s mop top-era teenage heartthrob. Gary has also gone the more traditional route as a fan-favorite Halloween monster, complete with green skin, suture marks, and neck bolts.

"I don't want to be the center of attention, but in my job, I know that at times I'm going to be," Gary said. "Halloween's not just about me. It's an enjoyable part of something our Company loves to do."

Across the Corporate Campus, Teams from different departments compete in producing the best Southwest-related skits, short films, walk-throughs, or family-friendly attractions. The grand prize is the coveted Golden Pumpkin that the winning department proudly displays until the next Halloween. Headquarters basically becomes an amusement park for the day, with haunted houses, kid-friendly fun, and Broadway-style shows. One year, the Finance Department turned the entire second floor into a pirate-themed ride, with rolling canoes, fog, and actual singing pirates.

In operational locations, Frontline Employees deck out ticket counters, gates, and Employee common areas with different themes and are encouraged to wear approved Halloween accessories.

No one at Southwest seems to recall how the love for Halloween got started, but as far back as 1972, Hostesses (now called Flight Attendants) dressed up for St. Patrick's Day and Easter (they were bunny rabbits). By the mid-1970s, Employees were definitely getting into the Halloween spirit.

"When I joined the Company in the 1980s, it was in full swing. You were just sort of expected to join in the fun," Gary said.

Herb loved celebrating the holiday with Employees, and over the years he had dressed up as the patriarch of a "spooky" fictional family, a dreamy doctor from a hit medical drama, and of course, everyone's favorite rock 'n' roll icon to impersonate.

↑
Herb and Gary celebrate Halloween in 2007.

"Herb set a really high bar when it comes to Halloween," Gary said.

As with everything at Southwest, there's a method to the madness. The Halloween celebrations not only help People enjoy what they do, they interrupt the routines and traditional thought processes and serve as the ultimate Team-building exercise. They encourage People to be more creative and to feel comfortable trying new things, and it's a day when Leaders step back and take direction from Employees.

After all, it's hard to cling to conventional wisdom when the head of the Company dresses as a female laundress from a hit Broadway musical.

↓
Gary Kelly, dressed as the iconic frontman of a popular Texas rock band, joins in the Halloween fun with Southwest Customer Service Agents Nellie Karenev and Maryann Rojas in 2008.

Queen of Hearts

In Colleen Barrett's family, cowbells were rung to celebrate great accomplishments, and by that measure, a carillon should have sounded on March 19, 2001. That was the date Southwest announced that she would become the first woman President of Southwest Airlines, or of any major U.S. airline for that matter.

She would go on to receive a host of accolades, including winning the Outstanding Woman in Aviation Award in 2007 and landing repeatedly on a prominent list of the 100 most powerful women in business.

Born poor in rural Vermont, Colleen earned a two-year associate degree and made her way to Texas, where in 1967 she became Herb Kelleher's legal secretary when the Southwest Founder was still working as a lawyer in San Antonio. She followed Herb to Southwest, assuming the role of Corporate Secretary in 1978. In 1986, she became Vice President Administration and, in 1990, Executive Vice President Customers. But she is best known as the architect of Southwest's Culture.

No one embodies Southwest's Culture and Values more than Colleen Barrett.

SWA®
SOUTHWEST AIRLINES®

Under Colleen's Leadership, Southwest's Culture became a key engine for the Company's growth.

In many ways, Colleen was the perfect complement to Herb. He could provide the determination, competitiveness, and military lingo to rally the troops. She reminded everyone to treat others with respect and to follow The Golden Rule, which her mother had instilled in her when she was growing up. The result was a Culture that could be both fierce and kind at the same time.

"Herb enjoys the persona of the disorganized mad scientist; she's the organizer," Chairman and CEO Gary Kelly said.

"They formed a very powerful partnership in that way." But by playing such a prominent role in the Company at a time when few women held leadership positions in corporate America, Colleen also gave Southwest something many businesses lacked: a feminine side.

"Southwest enjoys a real femininity as a Company that's really healthy," Gary said. "We're very comfortable using the word 'love.' We're very comfortable hugging because we want to think of each other as Family. And I think she gets a lot of that credit."

Colleen's Leadership has been an inspiration to others both inside and outside the Company and has reinforced Southwest's efforts to promote women into Leadership positions.

"One of the Leaders who's had the most impact on me as I've grown up inside the organization has been Colleen," said Linda Rutherford, Executive Vice President People & Communications and Chief Communications Officer.

As of 2019, more than 40 percent of Southwest's Employees and about 30 percent of Executives were women. In addition to Colleen, the Company has a long history of promoting female Executives, including Laura Wright, who took over as Senior Vice President Finance & Chief Financial Officer after Gary became CEO in 2004. Laura remained CFO until 2012 as one of the most tenured and powerful women in airline finance. She was succeeded by Tammy Romo, who remains Executive Vice President & CFO.

Donna Conover, who joined the Company in 1977, became Vice President Inflight Services & Provisioning in 1998, and later held roles such as Executive Vice President Customer Service and Executive Vice President Customer Operations. Other women in Senior Executive positions include Ginger Hardage, who joined Southwest in 1990 and retired in 2017 as Senior Vice President Culture & Communications; Joyce Rogge, who started with Southwest in 1988 as Manager of Promotions and retired in 2006 as Senior Vice President Marketing; and Linda, who started with Southwest in 1992.

Southwest has taken other steps to promote gender diversity. In 2018, for example, the Company awarded $25,000 in scholarships to women for additional flight training and assistance in obtaining pilots' licenses. It also awarded scholarships to women for Aviation Maintenance Professional Certification to pursue careers as aviation maintenance professionals.

In 2016, Captain Nicole Alicea and First Officer Nicole Sturrett made history when they became Southwest's first African American female Pilot Crew. Making history wasn't anything new for Alicea, who joined Southwest in 2002 as the Company's first African American woman Pilot. Her father was also a Southwest Pilot, and together they were the first African American father-daughter Flight Crew for any major airline.

While Southwest is known for its Culture, it also wants to be known for its inclusiveness, said Ellen Torbert, who retired in 2021 from her role as Vice President Diversity, Equity, & Inclusion. "It's about acknowledging the skills, unique perspectives, and experiences of all our Employees, and valuing them being their authentic selves. It's about the respect we show each other that fuels our unity to be the best that we can be."

Colleen retired in 2008 and was given the title President Emeritus. Gary dedicated a special airplane to her—named *Heroine of the Heart*—which remains a permanent member of the Southwest fleet. There was also an impromptu tribute in the Headquarters lobby that included a somewhat altered version of a famous country song—and of course, a lot of cowbells.

Nicole Alicea joined Southwest in 2002 as the Company's first Black female Pilot.

Kim
Ramirez
SOUTHWEST
Mother
Fernando
Ramirez
SOUTHWEST
Father
Jeremy
Ramirez
SOUTHWEST
Son

Family Ties

When Southwest Employees inspire the next generation of their family members to work for the airline, the Company sees it as a badge of honor.

Many companies have policies against hiring multiple members of the same family, but Southwest not only allows it, the airline encourages it as long as no conflict of interest exists. The Company works to include family members in events, and Employees periodically bring their children to work. Some of those children grow up to work for Southwest.

"It makes stronger Employees because they know the history; they've experienced it through their parents," said Kim Ramirez, who retired in 2016 as Senior Manager Administration. "They take that with them when they start working, and they understand where the Company came from."

Kim is something of an expert on the matter. She joined Southwest in 1986 in the Reservations Department, and her husband, Fernando, was hired three years later as a Ramp Agent. Five other members of their family—their three children, a daughter-in-law, and a niece—have all worked for Southwest.

"It's a very special thing," said son Jeremy, who joined in 2010. "The fact that one Company can [have] so many family members doing such a wide variety of things speaks volumes to Southwest's ability to bring in and retain talent and families as well."

Jeremy, the second-oldest child in the Ramirez family, got his flight dispatch license and joined Southwest in 2010, working in Pilot Crew Scheduling. Later he moved to Ground Operations and is currently working on the Schedule Development Team in Network Planning.

Kristina Ramirez Snyder, the oldest child, was the first of the Ramirez children to apply at Southwest. She had worked at several other places and wasn't happy. Kim said, "Well, why don't you try Southwest? At least you'll have good stability and room to grow."

In 2006, Kristina got hired in Customer Relations and later moved to Marketing. She worked at Southwest for more than 10 years before choosing to leave and stay at home with her children.

When her children were still little, Kim transferred to the ticket counter at Love Field. "She was working during the day shift, and I would work at night on the ramp," Fernando said. "I would take the kids and show up at the ticket counter. That way we didn't pay a babysitter that much."

For Kristina, those airport handoffs were some of her earliest memories of Southwest.

"I remember growing up around the Culture," she said. "They would take us up there, and I remember just running around at the airport.

"At that time, there was nothing over in that old terminal, so we would just play up there. In high school, [I went] to visit my mom one time, and they were all out in the parking lot doing a water balloon toss and just having a great old time. I was like, 'OK, I want to work here.'"

Robbie, the youngest son, joined Southwest in 2013, worked in Revenue Management, and later became a Marketing Analyst for the Rapid Rewards® Team. Like his brother and sister, he'd grown up in the Southwest Culture, so it was only fitting that he married another Employee. He met his future wife, Allison, at a gym near Southwest Headquarters in 2014. Allison had started in 2011 as a Communications Intern in Ground Operations, and Kim, who oversaw communications for Ground Operations by then, had hired her. "I already knew of [Robbie], and one day I casually said, 'Hey, this may sound strange, but I think I work for your mom!' The rest is history."

After they started dating, Allison took an Instructor position with Southwest Airlines University, SWAU, at Chicago (Midway), and they continued to date long-distance for a while. Robbie found a job working as a Cargo Agent on the overnight shift and moved to Chicago, giving up both a desk job and the warm Dallas weather. They got married in Key West in 2017 and received a card from Chairman and CEO Gary Kelly.

After several years of working the night shift, Robbie decided he wanted a better work-life balance. He trained to become a firefighter and paramedic and left the Company in April 2020. Allison, meanwhile, was recruited a month later to do training for a grocery retailer. She and Robbie still treasure their time at Southwest.

Robbie said that leaving the Company after almost 11 years was one of the hardest decisions he's ever made. "Your Coworkers are like your Family," he said. "I know when I was going through paramedic school and handling basically

Ramirez family members stand by the Wright Amendment Countdown Clock in 2014.

two jobs at once, I heavily relied on my Coworkers to help me out, cover my shifts. None of that would have been possible without them. Whether you're working with your actual blood family or your work Family, it's still Family."

The attraction to Southwest wasn't just limited to the Ramirez children. Caroline Snavely Sears, Kim's niece, studied marketing at the University of Texas and got hired in 2013 as an Intern in Cargo and Charters, which was part of Ground Operations at the time. Given the family's long association with Southwest, and the fact that Southwest frequently came up in case studies at UT, she knew where she wanted to work.

"Southwest is kind of like the Holy Grail when it comes to advertising and marketing," she said. "There are a lot of case studies and a lot of great things that Southwest does in the advertising space. And I've definitely had a lot of exposure to the Company through my family."

When Caroline was hired as an Intern, Kim was working in the same department. Kim and Caroline's time together in Ground Operations was one of the few times family members saw each other regularly at work.

"My desk was probably 20 feet away from hers, so it was a very good experience being in a corporate world, having your aunt take care of you just down the cubicle row," Caroline said. She was later hired full time in Marketing and transferred to the Southwest Business Department, before leaving the Company in 2021.

The Ramirez family not only grew up in Southwest's Culture, but they also understood the Southwest Spirit and the attitude the Company looks for in Employees. Over the years, family relationships have been a valuable recruiting tool for Southwest, one that helps perpetuate its Culture and Values from one generation to the next.

Kim and Fernando retired in 2016, and in 2020, they celebrated their 40th wedding anniversary. While there are fewer members of the Ramirez family at Southwest these days, they all still feel connected to it.

Will we see any more of the family working for the Company?

"Maybe the next generation, but it'll be awhile," Kristina said.

From Surviving to Thriving

Keeping an Eye on the Bottom Line

20
20
10
10
10
10
20
20

All's Fare in LUV and War

When a competitor tried to price Southwest out of the sky, it fought back with low fares—and free liquor.

When Southwest started flying on June 18, 1971, it sent a shockwave through the industry. On the same day as its maiden flight, its two biggest competitors, Braniff and Texas International, cut their fares—for the first time anyone could remember—to match Southwest's on competing routes.

Less than two years later, on February 1, 1973, Southwest President and CEO Lamar Muse was eating breakfast at his home and reading *The Dallas Morning News*. He turned a page in the newspaper and saw a full-page ad from Braniff with heavy block print announcing a "Get Acquainted Sale" in the Dallas-Houston market for $13—half the regular fare—that would end on April Fool's Day.

Braniff had been flying in Texas since the 1930s. The Dallas-Houston market was a small one for Braniff, but it was a vital artery for Southwest, and Braniff knew that if the upstart airline lost it, it would be out of business. Lamar called the Executives together and vowed to design his own newspaper ad to fight back.

As the staff meeting ended, Lamar's real estate agent called. The agent had been scheduled to show Lamar a new condominium that morning, but Lamar hadn't shown up. The agent told Lamar he understood, and then he pointed out that savings and loans had for years won new accounts by giving away gifts, such as toasters or waffle irons, to new depositors.

Lamar liked the idea. But what should Southwest give away? Most of its Customers at the time were businessmen, and its "Hostesses"—as it referred to Flight Attendants back then—served a lot of liquor. Why not offer a free bottle of booze, preferably ones that cost no more than $13? Lamar figured that Customers on an expense account would keep paying the $26 fare just to get the free liquor. The Company stocked up on Chivas Regal Scotch, Crown Royal Canadian Whisky, and Smirnoff Vodka. (Teetotalers got a leather-lined ice bucket.)

Then, Lamar drafted an ad of his own—this one would be *two* pages. The first said, in big, bold print:

"Nobody's going to shoot Southwest Airlines out of the sky for a lousy $13."

The second page explained that while Southwest would match Braniff's $13 fare, anyone who paid the full $26 ticket price would get a nice gift. The ad also pointed out that the only reason Braniff was cutting its fares was because of Southwest, and if travelers wanted to continue to have low fares and good service, they should support the new carrier.

Southwest ran the ad in the four newspapers in Dallas and Houston and had 50,000 color brochures printed and delivered them to downtown office buildings in each city. Off-duty Pilots and Hostesses, in uniform, handed them out on street corners during the noon hour.

The efforts paid off. By the end of February 1973, Southwest's average number of Customers increased 117 percent from a year earlier, and its average load increased 152 percent. Company Executives noticed something else that would be very important: Those gains came with three planes instead of four—Southwest had sold the fourth of its original 737s by then—which meant its average cost per Customer had declined by 56 percent.

Of course, Braniff did not accept defeat gracefully. During the promotion, Herb Kelleher got a call from someone claiming to be from the Texas Alcoholic Beverage Commission. The commission, the caller said, had received complaints that giving away so much free booze was exerting undue temptation on born-again travelers.

"I suspect," Herb replied, "that the complaining organization begins with a 'B' that does not stand for 'Baptist.' Isn't that so?"

"That is so," the caller said sheepishly, and hung up.

In late February, Lamar got a call from Houston financier Fayez Sarofim. "Lamar," he said, "I flew your airline up to Dallas this morning, and they gave me a bottle of Chivas Regal. And when I came back this afternoon, they gave me another bottle of Chivas Regal. That's class, Lamar! Besides that, both flights were full. I smell money, Lamar, and I'm going to start buying your stock." Within a couple of months, Fayez became Southwest's second-largest Shareholder.

Far from being blown out of the sky, the promotion resulted in Southwest's first monthly net profit, in March 1973. It was the last time the Company would lose money on a quarterly basis until the first quarter of 1987.

Over the years, Southwest has had many other successful promotions, but it was the Company's original fare sale in 1973 that set the tone and sent a message to competitors that in any fare war, Southwest would fight to win.

After a competitor slashed fares to $13 in 1973, Southwest fought back by matching the discount and offering a free bottle of liquor to Customers who paid full price. Far from being blown out of the sky, the promotion resulted in Southwest's first monthly net profit.

Taking Stock—and Giving It

Even though Southwest received its operating certificate in 1971, gaining the legal right to fly was only part of the battle. Herb Kelleher's pressing question to Rollin King back in 1966 continued to hang over the Company as it struggled to begin operations—"Where will we get the capital?"

By going public, Southwest's stock became an important currency for both Shareholders and Employees, who have been rewarded handsomely over the years.

After Lamar Muse became President and CEO, he developed a plan that included issuing $1.25 million worth of debentures (essentially debt that could be converted into common stock once it was issued), which he called "walking-around money." Next, he wanted to file for a public stock offering that would raise at least $6 million, and he wanted to do it before Southwest started flying. He knew the airline might not be profitable in its first year, and if Investors saw it was losing money, they would be less likely to buy the stock.

But before Southwest could even get that far, Braniff once again butted in. Stock offerings require brokerage firms to underwrite the offering, and in Southwest's case, it was counting on a Dallas firm to be one of the underwriters. The firm refused, and some of the Investors who'd bought Southwest's debentures worried that without a local firm participating in the offering, it would fail.

SOUTHWEST AIRLINES
SOUTHWEST AIRLINES CO.
TRANSFERABLE IN NEW YORK, NEW YORK AND DALLAS, TEXAS
SPECIMEN
SHARES OF COMMON STOCK OF THE PAR VALUE OF $1.00 EACH OF
SOUTHWEST AIRLINES CO.
by duly authorized attorney upon surrender of this Certificate properly endorsed.
all the provisions of the Articles of Incorporation of the Corporation, as now or hereafter amended
the Transfer Agent and Registrar.
signatures of its duly authorized officers.
CUSIP 844741 10 8
SOUTHWEST AIRLINES CO.
T E X A S
SECRETARY

After some supersleuthing, Lamar learned that the Dallas firm was underwriting the bonds for the new Dallas/Fort Worth Regional Airport (DFW)—a massive bond deal worth millions, far more than Southwest's little stock offering. Braniff's CEO told the firm's executives that if they participated in Southwest's offering, he would make sure they wouldn't see a nickel from the DFW deal. (Braniff was the biggest carrier that would be based at the new airport, so the Braniff CEO had a lot of influence.)

Lamar flew to New York and found another underwriter, Model Roland & Co., to agree to serve as a principal underwriter along with Thomson McKinnon & Auchincloss Inc., which already owned some of the debentures. The addition of Model Roland eased Investors' concerns, and the offering was back on track.

Southwest's shares began trading over the counter—meaning they weren't listed on a major exchange—on June 8, 1971, just 10 days before the airline started flying. The Company sold 650,000 shares at $11 apiece, raising $6.5 million. Four years later, Southwest was admitted to the American Stock Exchange, which required a ticker symbol. (The Company didn't need a ticker for trading over the counter.) The obvious symbols—"S," "SW," "SWA"—were already taken. Lamar suggested "LUV," reflecting the Company's home base of Love Field as well as the Company's early love-themed marketing slogans:

"There's somebody else up there who loves you," and "Spreading love all over Texas."

Southwest migrated to the more prestigious New York Stock Exchange in 1977.

The stock gave the Company access to an important currency. And as soon as it turned its first profit in 1973, it launched its ProfitSharing Plan—the first in the industry—allowing Employees to participate in the Company's financial success. Southwest remained profitable on an annual basis for the next 46 years, an achievement no other airline can claim.

↓

Southwest's retirement plans (including 401(k) and ProfitSharing) are a generous way for Employees to prepare for the future.

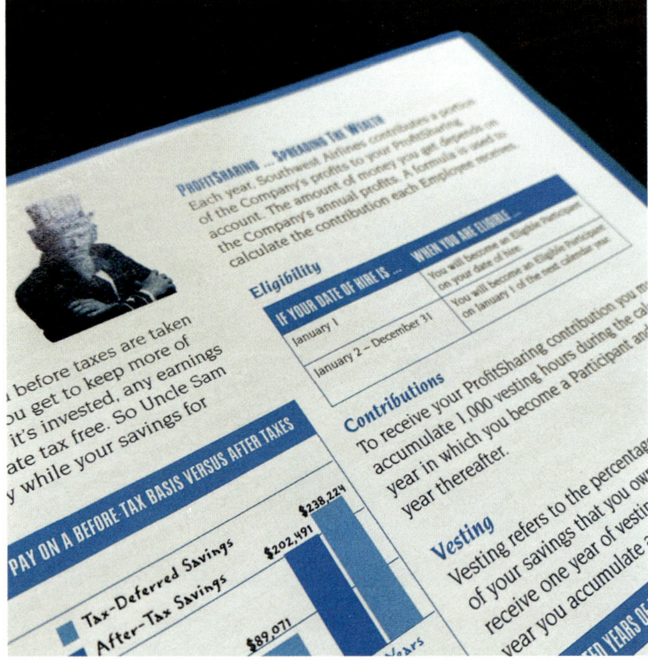

With ProfitSharing and stock awards, Employees have shared in Southwest's success. As one of the only airlines that Wall Street considered a growth stock, the Company's financial performance meant Employees, as well as Investors, reaped the rewards. Since its inception, Southwest Airlines ProfitSharing has distributed almost $6 billion to Employees.

"From a business point of view, [Herb] needed to have People who were motivated to do the right thing for his Customers. And from a People point of view, [ProfitSharing] was a perfect thing, [a] perfect way for him to reinforce [that message]," Board Member and former Chief Financial Officer John Denison said. "It also became a key tool in maintaining good labor relations. ... One of the key decisions [was avoiding] a track that said that the unions wouldn't be a part of the Company."

Southwest's strong performance enabled it to reach Employees through ProfitSharing and stock ownership that would allow them "to share the benefits of the Company as we go forward," he added. "That's been the history of the Company."

Larry Dzieranowski, who started as a Ramp Agent in San Antonio in 1975 and was still with the Company until passing away in early 2021, said in a 2020 interview that he remembered getting stock options in the early days. "I didn't even know what stock was or what a share was," he said. "I had mine through every one of those splits," referring to the 14 times Southwest stock has split. "It's been a real good thing."

Particularly in the 1980s when hostile takeovers were common in the airline industry, Southwest has always been protective of its ownership structure. Herb knew that losing control of the Company would mean losing control of the Culture and ultimately jeopardize Southwest's success. That's why Herb threatened a "scorched earth" policy toward potential takeovers.

A young investment banker once showed up in his office suggesting the Company would be a juicy takeover target. Herb rose from his desk, backed the banker against the wall, and lectured him on how Russia had destroyed its own property rather than allow it to be taken over by the Nazis during World War II. "Anybody who buys this Company is going to have ashes, soot, and cinders!" Herb yelled. The man ran from Herb's office, glasses askew.

"What happened?" asked Colleen Barrett, who was Corporate Secretary, looking up from her desk.

"I just sent a message to Wall Street," Herb said.

He sent another message with the Company's 1986 Annual Report to Shareholders. In the 1980s, the proliferation of discount carriers had led to a wave of consolidations. He was determined to keep Southwest independent. He ordered a cover for the report—all black, with yellow letters that read, "In 1986 we didn't merge."

What Herb understood was that the Company's value came from its People. That has proven true time and again. Accounting for stock splits, Southwest's shares have soared from 22 cents at the beginning of 1980, to a high of $66.29 in early 2018. In 2020, before the COVID-19 pandemic, the Company's stock was trading above $58. Herb's belief in putting "Employees first, then Customers" is very good for Shareholders, as well.

Conquering the Cost Mountain

Southwest has always kept a keen eye on its costs, and over the years, that's added up to a lot more than peanuts.

From the beginning, keeping costs low was a matter of survival at Southwest. It didn't do things the way other airlines did. It eschewed debt, offered no first-class service, and structured its route map so Customers could fly where they wanted to go rather than forcing them to connect through hubs. And, of course, there were the peanuts. Its flights were short, so it didn't offer meals, just a small package of snacks that became a part of its image.

Keeping costs low meant Southwest could keep fares low, which drew more Customers. As if to remind its People of this relationship, every paycheck Employees receive includes the words "Deposits made possible by your Southwest Customers."

"You are involved in a crusade," Founder Herb Kelleher used to tell Employees.

The sense that they were all in the fight together became a strength. When the Company planned a major expansion, it asked its People to embrace austerity measures even more than they already did. And when times were tough, everyone pulled together and found new ways to save money and be more efficient.

Southwest

Using a single aircraft type and focusing, in the early days, on secondary airports also saved money, as did the flexibility of its People.

As it learned with the development of the 10-Minute Turn, sometimes the things Southwest did out of necessity became competitive advantages. Other times, it was the creativity of its People and their relentless commitment to keep costs low. The savings weren't always obvious outside the Company, but internally, they were—and still are—a constant focus. In the late 1970s, when Howard Putnam became President and CEO, Southwest's cost per available seat mile was about half that of its rivals. "Rather than taking the attitude that we could relax and be a little less frugal, we continued to run the Company as if our good fortunes could turn around any second—which, of course, they could," Howard said.

Soon after he arrived, Howard asked then-Vice President Flight Operations Don Ogden about his budget. Don, who was known as "Captain O," had flown 707s for another airline before retiring and joining Southwest as one of the "Over the Hill Gang"—a seasoned bunch of senior Executives brought in by original President and CEO Lamar Muse to get the Company off the ground. Don smoked a pipe, and when Howard asked him about the budget, Don leaned back in his chair, blew a big puff of smoke, and said, "Howard, we don't have a budget. We only spend money when we have to."

Over the years, as the Company grew bigger and its finances became more complex, it adopted more formal budgeting processes, but Don's view about spending remained. Not only did the Company only do it when it had to, it constantly looked for ways big and small to keep its expenses low.

↑
In a special ceremony, aircraft N68SW is christened *The Winning Spirit* and dedicated to Southwest's Original Employees as part of the Company's 10th anniversary on June 18, 1981. From left are Herb, Bill Franklin, Rollin King, Don Ogden, and Jack Vidal.

In the 1990s, when the Company needed 800 new computers for its reservation center in Albuquerque, it considered the major PC makers of the day, but former Director Technical Services Mike Golden had a better idea. "We had a big internal debate over which computer from the three main technology companies at the time would be the official standard at Southwest Airlines," former CEO Jim Parker said. "Mike Golden and his Technical Services Department said, 'Well, we can buy the box; we can buy the parts; we can put the parts together; and we can do all that for about half of what it would cost to buy the PCs.'" The group of Employees, which became known as "Mike's Tronics," volunteered to work on an ad hoc assembly line. They bought parts at various wholesalers, and Employees put them together. Mike's ingenuity, and the collective Team Spirit of its People, saved Southwest about $1 million on new computers (or more than $2 million in 2021 dollars).

In 2000, Southwest reduced the number of peanuts in each package by three, which saved $300,000.

During the days when computer monitors had cathode-ray tubes, the Company encouraged Employees to turn off their screens before they left work to save on electricity.

Over the years, Southwest Employees found other ways to save the Company money. In one instance, a Ramp Agent recommended that they stop ordering custom mop heads for galley cleaning. In another, a Flight Attendant said if the Company used regular bags to collect cups and other recyclable items on the planes, it could save money by not having custom-printed bags that said "Southwest Recycles," which, after all, was sort of obvious since they were collecting recyclables in the first place.

Southwest is still on the lookout for savings. In 2019, its Corporate Facilities Team replaced light poles at its Headquarters campus. The new poles use LED lights, which improved safety and exterior lighting quality while using less energy, saving $10,000 a month.

The Company's Facilities and Technology Teams recently began testing a new tool at Dallas (Love Field) designed to improve gate efficiency and reduce equipment repair, maintenance costs, and aircraft fuel consumption. The tool uses real-time data to measure Ground Power Unit (GPU) and Pre-Conditioned Air (PCA) use by the aircraft. Based on the test results, Southwest expects to save as much as $400,000 in annual fuel consumption at each airport using the new tool—and those savings may grow over time. The tests have been expanded to Los Angeles (LAX), Phoenix, and Houston (Hobby).

Meanwhile, Southwest's Technology Team migrated data to the new Southwest Data Center (WNDC). The migration wrapped up in 2020 and reduced the Company's footprint and power consumption by more than 50 percent. It also reduced the amount of computing infrastructure it needs, lowering equipment costs and reducing maintenance. Southwest expects to save more than $6 million over seven years.

While it's always looking to reduce costs internally, sometimes the higher costs come from outside. In 1997, for example, rival airlines convinced Congress to change the taxes for air tickets from a flat 10 percent to one that was levied on each flight segment. The result penalized short-haul carriers—namely Southwest. It responded by accelerating plans to incorporate more long-haul flights into its schedule. "People said we could not do long-haul because the longer you fly, the less you can differentiate your costs, so Southwest loses its cost advantage over the other carriers, but what they are forgetting," Herb said at the time, "is that costs decline the longer you fly."

What its rivals might not have understood was that keeping its costs low wasn't just about how far Southwest flew; it was about its commitment to the crusade.

Gas Money

At Southwest Airlines, Employees don't have to wait to be told what to do. When they see a need or a challenge, they are encouraged to look for solutions and bring all ideas to the table. This from-the-ground-up ingenuity took center stage in October 1990, when, in the face of soaring fuel costs, the Company's Employees chipped in to buy gas.

That summer, jet fuel prices rose sharply, in large part because of Iraq's invasion of Kuwait. By the end of August, the price of crude oil had surged more than 75 percent in less than three months, and jet fuel prices more than doubled, from about 50 cents a gallon to more than a dollar.

To offset such a sudden increase in one of the Company's biggest expenses, Matt Buckley, who started with Southwest in 1982 as a Ramp Agent in Midland/Odessa and later became Vice President Cargo & Charters, proposed allowing Employees to purchase jet fuel for $1.10 a gallon using payroll deductions. Employees on the ground encouraged others to join in. Eventually, about one-third of the 8,600 Employees at the time contributed to what became known as the Fuel from the Heart program.

When oil prices soared in 1990, Southwest's Employees pitched in by donating from their hard-earned paychecks.

OF AMERICA
J50848839B

In all, Fuel from the Heart raised about $130,000. Although it didn't make a big dent in the Company's fuel bill, it was an important symbolic gesture.

"It was reflective of how this was a shared battle," said retired Senior Vice President Business Development Dave Ridley. "So, Fuel from the Heart was spectacular."

It was one more example of how Southwest leads from within and how innovation can come from anywhere regardless of someone's title. After all, the program wasn't started by top management. Herb, who was Chairman, President, and CEO then, didn't even know about it until later, and he only learned of the effort when he received a banner signed by all the Employees who'd pledged part of their paychecks.

"It wasn't so much the money as the attitude that I loved," Herb said. "It indicated that the Spirit of Southwest Airlines was alive."

Fuel from the Heart is just one example of how, over the years, Southwest Employees have rallied around causes in support of the Company and their fellow Employees. The Southwest Airlines Employee Catastrophic Assistance Charity, which had its beginnings in 1983 and was formalized as an official nonprofit organization in 1990, let Employees volunteer for payroll deductions to be donated to fellow Employees dealing with catastrophic illness or events in their lives. After Hurricane Katrina in August 2005, Employees used deductions to make donations to help their Coworkers impacted by the devastation. The Company teamed up with the Red Cross, in addition to the Employee Catastrophic Program, and matched Employee donations dollar-for-dollar.

No matter what challenges come Southwest's way, the determination and dedication demonstrated by the Fuel from the Heart program lives on.

→

Southwest Employees put a lot of Heart into everything they do, and the Heart livery was designed to reflect that. Here, Operational Employees get a first look at the new livery in August 2014, one month before its public unveiling.

The Hedge Edge

In 1989, Southwest's annual revenue surpassed $1 billion, which meant it finally was considered a "major" airline. It arrived in the big leagues as some of the most venerated names in the industry were struggling. Iraq's invasion of Kuwait in 1990 had sent oil prices soaring and added about $3 billion to the industry's costs in just six months.

Between December 1990 and January 1992, four major competitors—Continental Airlines, Pan Am World Airways, Eastern Airlines, and Trans World Airlines—filed for bankruptcy. Many inside and outside the industry began to question whether deregulation had been a good idea.

For Southwest, the industry's struggles created opportunity, and it was the beginning of a decade in which the Company would redefine air travel on a national scale. It wasn't immune to the economic impact of higher fuel prices, however. Every penny increase for a gallon of jet fuel added about $3.1 million a year, or $260,000 a month, to its costs. At the end of 1990, it reported a quarterly loss, yet it still made money on an annual basis, which set it apart from the rest of the industry. The cover of its Annual Report that year had a simple message from Founder Herb Kelleher: "In 1990, we made a profit."

Southwest utilized a brilliant strategy for reducing one of its biggest costs—jet fuel.

QTY TEST
FUEL QTY
FUEL QTY
FUEL QTY
CTR

At the same time, Southwest was expanding. It added flights to places such as Louisville, San Jose, California, and Baltimore/Washington (BWI) in 1993, and announced plans to be Boeing's launch customer for the new 737 Next Generation series with the purchase of 63 737-700s. As an exclamation mark to everything that set the Company apart, Southwest consistently led the industry in key customer service metrics tracked by the U.S. Department of Transportation: best ontime performance, fewest mishandled bags, and fewest customer complaints. In fact, the Company led these categories so frequently, it dubbed the designation the industry's "Triple Crown," an award Southwest gave itself. (By 1997, Southwest had achieved the "Triple Crown" for more than 30 months.)

↓
Southwest Mechanics supervise the fueling of a 737-700 prior to a test flight from Dallas (Love Field) in 1997.

The difference between Southwest's performance and the rest of the industry caused everyone to take notice. "The media attention, the political attention, the investment community attention, the attention from our competition—it was just absolutely extraordinary," recalled Chairman and CEO Gary Kelly, who was Chief Financial Officer at the time. "It became all about Southwest, you know, and how is Southwest doing so well and everybody else is doing so poorly, and why doesn't everybody else do what Southwest does?"

One thing the Company didn't do was rest on its laurels.

Herb embraced the philosophy that "we manage in good times so that all of us will be protected from bad times."

With that in mind and seeing the struggles of competitors in the early 1990s, Gary began examining one of Southwest's key potential vulnerabilities: jet fuel prices. Fuel is one of the Company's biggest expenses (second only to Southwest's largest cost category: salaries, wages, and benefits), and in 1993, its fuel costs rose to $304.4 million from $230.2 million in 1991—an increase of 33 percent.

In 1994, Gary met with Barry Siler, a commodities trading consultant in Houston, and together they developed a program to hedge the cost of jet fuel. A hedge is a financial instrument to reduce risk, much like an insurance policy. For example, the Company might enter a futures contract that gave it the option to buy or sell crude oil or other energy products by a certain date at a certain price. Southwest then used the proceeds from those transactions to offset the higher cost of jet fuel.

The tactic could save money, but it also gave Southwest greater predictability for fuel costs.

Gary and Barry started small with the hedging program, locking in prices for only about 20 to 30 percent of the Company's fuel needs no more than six months in advance. As the program began working, Gary expanded it, bringing it in-house in 1998. He later enlisted the help of Scott Topping, a young associate in the Finance Department who would later become Treasurer. Oil prices fell dramatically in the late 1990s, and Gary, Scott, and the rest of the Fuel Management Department were able to lock in prices at about 35 cents a gallon.

Their timing was perfect. In 1999, the price of crude oil more than doubled, to $26.10 a barrel in December from $12.50 in January, and it kept going, reaching $34 almost a year later. Yet, Southwest was paying as much as 40 percent less for fuel than some of its rivals who hadn't hedged. In January 2001, *The Wall Street Journal* called the Company's hedging program "state-of-the-art" and said it was unmatched by competitors. Six months earlier, Gary had hedged all of Southwest's jet fuel purchases—every drop of fuel it bought—as prices rose. The move saved $43.1 million in the third quarter of 2000 alone and boosted net income by 45 percent over the previous year.

The strategy helped the Company remain profitable during the lean years after the 9/11 terror attacks, and it provided a competitive advantage as oil prices soared to more than $147 a barrel in 2008. By then, hedging had saved the Company $3.5 billion during the previous decade, equal to about 83 percent of its profit during that time.

During the Great Recession of 2008, Southwest used hedges to buy 70 percent of its jet fuel based on $51-a-barrel oil prices, rather than the $130-a-barrel-equivalent rivals were paying. The savings allowed the Company to avoid charging fees for the first two checked bags within weight and size limits and other services that many of its competitors adopted.

Southwest continues to strategically hedge jet fuel purchases, and the program insulates it from sudden, catastrophic price fluctuations. It also helped fund the Company's growth, first across the country, then into international markets. Hedging played a key role not just in getting Southwest into the majors, but in helping it swing for the fences.

Saving Gas

Like most airlines, jet fuel is one of Southwest's biggest expenses, and like most expenses, Southwest is always looking for ways to reduce it. In addition to the savings from its unparalleled hedging program, the Company has used a combination of technology and strategy to keep fuel costs as low as possible.

From the tips of its wings to the Heart of its flight schedules, Southwest is always looking for ways to reduce fuel costs.

Southwest launched a concentrated cross-departmental effort in 2010 focused on reducing fuel consumption, which included modernizing the fleet, examining all aspects of fuel usage, adding fleet enhancements such as winglets, reducing aircraft weight, and improving the efficiency of planning flights and operating aircraft, all in support of the Company's goal to further reduce its carbon footprint.

In 2013, Southwest hired Jeff Darnell from American Airlines and put him to work on initiatives that would continue the Company's cross-departmental efforts to improve fuel efficiency. As Manager Fuel Operations Performance in Network Operations Control (NOC), Jeff reviewed all fuel-related aspects of Southwest's operation, including how the Company planned and operated the aircraft.

One of the first things that caught Jeff's eye as he reviewed the flight planning system was the high amount of fuel planned for aircraft as they taxied out. After further analysis, it became clear that the system was calculating taxi-out fuel to the runway at a rate of 50 pounds per minute versus Boeing's recommended amount of 25. Once this excess was discovered and reduced, the result was savings of more than $4 million in 2013 and more than $6 million in 2014. And it didn't stop there. From 2013 to 2020, this cross-departmental efficiency effort returned an accumulated savings of more than $800 million.

Network Operations Control isn't the only place Southwest looks for savings. As Senior Director Fuel Supply Chain Management, Michael AuBuchon and his Team are responsible for fuel purchases, getting that purchased fuel to airports, and managing it until it enters the aircraft. Unlike many other airlines, Southwest buys directly from refineries and handles the shipping to the airports, rather than using a third party, which gives it more flexibility in negotiating contracts and saves about $50 million a year. It also allows the Team to get creative. In 2019, Southwest imported jet fuel for the first time ever to Los Angeles from

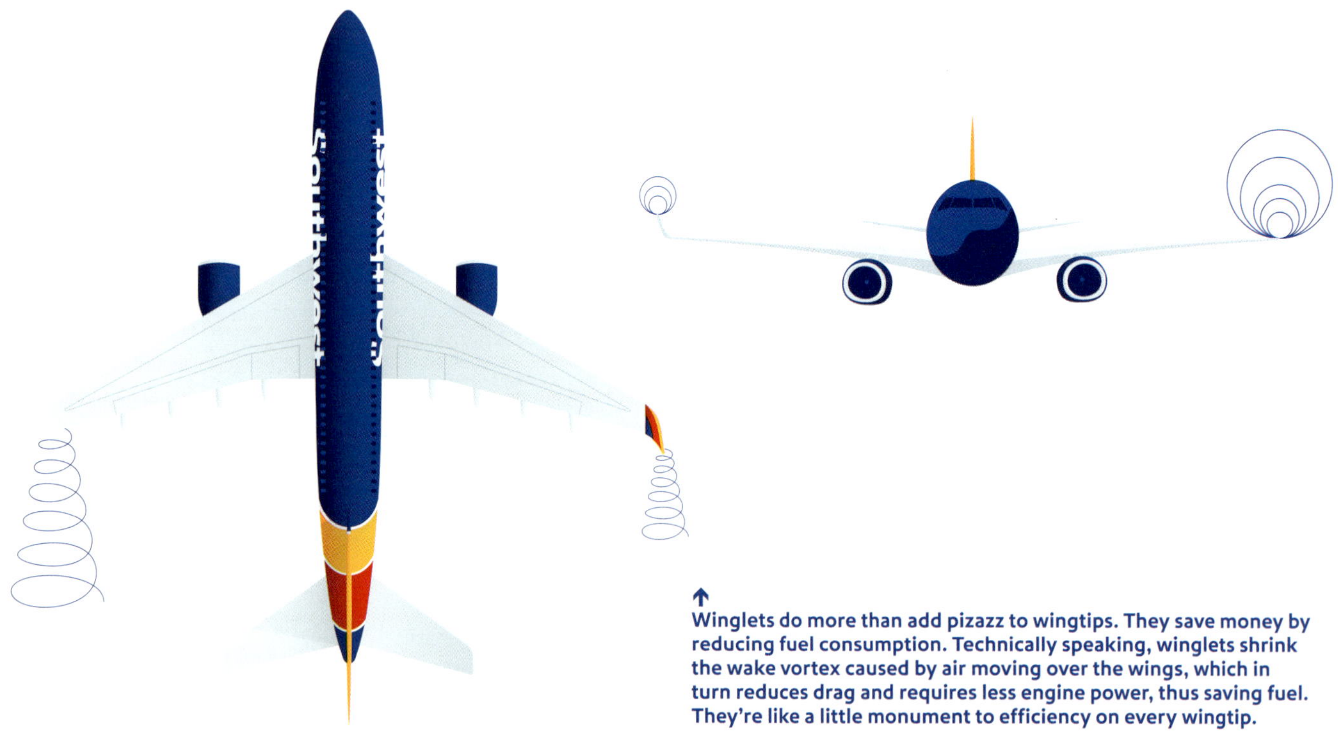

↑
Winglets do more than add pizazz to wingtips. They save money by reducing fuel consumption. Technically speaking, winglets shrink the wake vortex caused by air moving over the wings, which in turn reduces drag and requires less engine power, thus saving fuel. They're like a little monument to efficiency on every wingtip.

South Korea, which added liquidity to the market, lowered prices, and gave Southwest a competitive advantage.

Southwest also looks at innovative ways to reduce the cost of shipping fuel to airports. It recently began buying line space on pipelines versus transporting fuel by trucks, reducing costs by $1 million in 2019 alone. With lower jet fuel demand during the COVID-19 crisis, the Company used its pipeline space for a few months to ship gasoline for a refining company—earning a few hundred thousand dollars in the process.

In addition, Michael's Team works closely with the NOC to balance fuel inventories with fuel costs at Southwest's airports—including buying more fuel where it's less expensive and taking less fuel where it's more expensive.

"We find the sweet spot between the cost to carry that extra fuel and the price differential" of the fuel, Jeff said. The Company does about 4,000 of these logistics movements daily, and it has software that helps purchase fuel at 50 different locations and manage inventory at 120 others.

Southwest never stops looking for ways to reduce fuel consumption, from adjusting idle speeds on ground vehicle engines, to using ground electric power when planes are at the gate, to routine washing of jet engines to remove grime. Cleaner engines reduce fuel burn and emissions, and that, in turn, benefits the environment.

Since 2002, the Company has invested more than $620 million in fuel efficiency efforts. Perhaps the most visible example of this investment are the winglets that adorn the wingtips of Southwest jets. In 2003, the Company introduced Blended Winglets, which turn upward at the end of the wing and extend aircraft range and reduce fuel use, noise, and maintenance costs. In 2014, Southwest added Split Scimitar Winglets to its 737-800s. The new design improves the existing Blended Winglet, adding a ventral strake below the wing to help stabilize airflow. The winglets increase fuel savings from the 3.5 percent per plane for the Blended Winglet to as much as 5.5 percent per plane.

Southwest's focus on reducing fuel cost goes hand in hand with its efforts to reduce emissions—and with its efforts to develop sustainable aviation fuels. In 2014, the Company signed an agreement with Red Rocks Biofuels LLC to purchase about 3 million gallons a year of low-carbon renewable jet fuel, made using forest residues that will help reduce the risk of destructive wildfires in the western United States.

While work is still underway to make sustainable aviation fuel (SAF) a viable alternative to conventional jet fuel, Michael and his Team are optimistic about the future of SAF.

"We are a Company [that's] about pursuing the lowest cost possible to democratize the skies but that must be done in an environmentally responsible way to the greatest extent possible."

And that means Michael, Jeff, and their Teams are always looking for new ways to keep one of Southwest's biggest expenses as low as possible.

Winning with Customers

Doing the Right Thing

Low fares.
No hidden fees.
That's Transfarency.®

The Crowning Achievement: Customer Service

Sometimes the best awards are the ones you give yourself. In the days after deregulation, the U.S. Department of Transportation started tracking data on U.S. carriers' domestic operations, including key customer service metrics: best ontime performance, fewest mishandled bags, and fewest customer complaints. In May 1988, Southwest became the first airline to lead in all three categories. By 1990, the Company was at the top of all three categories so often, it dubbed the designation the industry's "Triple Crown."

One of the Triple Crown's pillars—fewest customer complaints—reflects Southwest's commitment to Positively Outrageous Service. The Company's history is full of examples.

Sometimes, Customer Service is as simple as helping to find a lost item. In February 2020, an executive for a large company left her tablet on a flight. She needed it for an important board presentation later that day. After she contacted Southwest, the Company located the tablet in less than an hour and coordinated with the executive to arrange delivery of the device.

When you're tops in all three major DOT airline metrics, a little recognition is in order. That's why Southwest invented the Triple Crown.

Number 1 Customer Satisfaction
TRIPLE CROWN

Sometimes, reuniting Customers with lost items is more involved. In early 2021, a 2-year-old boy traveling with his parents lost his beloved astronaut action figure. The boy's mother told her son the astronaut was on a "special mission," and planned to buy him a replacement when they got home.

The plane the family flew to Dallas went on to Little Rock, where a Southwest Operations Agent found the toy, which had the boy's name written on the sole of the astronaut's boot. The Operations Agent checked the flight's Passenger list and tracked the boy's parents down at their home. The boy's mother told him the story of the astronaut's "special mission," and when a Ramp Agent saw the toy and heard the story of the special mission, he decided to document the astronaut's endeavors. He took the action figure to the tarmac and snapped pictures of it in front of a plane, in the cowling of a jet engine, and in the cockpit. The Ramp Agent then wrote a letter, from the astronaut, detailing the mission. He decorated a box, put the letter, the photos, and the action figure inside and shipped it, at his own expense, to the boy.

When the boy's mother opened the box, she broke down in tears. She returned the favor, sending a video of the boy reunited with his favorite toy. When the Ramp Agent saw the video, *he* teared up.

Southwest has always empowered Employees to do whatever they think is necessary to help Customers. On a weekend in 1996, for example, a Customer flying for a transplant missed the last flight of the evening. "The duty manager chartered a plane and flew that Customer," said Donna Conover, who was Vice President Customer Service at the time. "That was a $10,000 decision made over a weekend, and the manager felt very comfortable making that kind of choice."

In other cases, Employees just do what—ahem—suits them. When a young attorney arrived in Albany, New York, just before midnight, he realized his garment bag didn't make the connection with the rest of his luggage. The bag contained his suit, which he needed for a swearing-in ceremony before the New York State Bar at 9 a.m. the next morning.

Customer Service Agent Claudia Ricci, who was working the overnight shift in the Baggage Service Office, came up with a unique solution. She thought the lawyer looked to be about the same size as Airport Operations Agent Luis "Louie" Gonzalez. She asked Louie if he would let the man borrow a suit. Louie agreed.

When their shift ended at 7 a.m., Claudia and Louie rushed to Louie's house to grab his suit—the only one he owned. Louie frantically searched his closet, but all he could find was a dress shirt and the suit jacket, not the pants. The only other dress pants he owned were the ones he'd been wearing at work, and they didn't match the suit. With the clock ticking, he and Claudia decided the pants were close enough to make do, so he changed pants and he and Claudia rushed the mismatched outfit to the lawyer's hotel room with a half hour to spare. (Talk about an ontime arrival!) The attorney made it to the ceremony, becoming the newest member of the bar—mismatched pants and all.

All of these examples prove what Colleen has always said about Southwest:

"We are in the Customer Service business; we just happen to fly airplanes."

↑ *Triple Crown One* taxis to the gate at Houston (Hobby) in 2018.

Open Seating

From its earliest days, Southwest did things differently. One of the first traditional airline practices it shunned was assigned seating. Since most of its flights were short, and because it needed to get its planes in the air quickly, it was just easier to let Customers find their own seats.

Open seating fit with the Company's egalitarian approach to air travel—one class of cabin, no meals, and, back then, everyone on the flight paid the same fare. The seating, like most other aspects of how Southwest operated in those days, reflected Founder Herb Kelleher's personality. He eschewed titles and bureaucracy, and he believed in treating everyone fairly. It seemed only fitting that Customers on Southwest would board on a first-come, first-served basis. If they were new to Southwest, or seemed to be confused about where to sit, Flight Attendants might remind them, "You can sit anywhere you want—just like at church."

Because all the fares on the flight were the same, Customers initially took the receipt from the ticket purchase and exchanged it at the gate for a boarding pass. Later, additional fare levels were introduced, and in the 1980s, the Company adopted its famous colorful plastic boarding passes, which Operations Agents collected from Customers and reused.

From plastic boarding passes to steel stanchions, Southwest's boarding process has always been a bit different—and highly efficient.

1-5
6-10
16-20

↑
Southwest's reusable plastic boarding passes, introduced in the early 1980s, were a hallmark of the Company's boarding procedure until they were discontinued in 2002.

Southwest has tweaked the boarding system over the years. In 2002, it commissioned the testing of dual jet bridges in Austin, Albany, and Dallas (Love Field). Customers walking down the jet bridge came to a fork, where they could choose to board through the front or the back of the plane. While it shaved a few minutes off turnaround times, the savings weren't enough to justify the costs. Moreover, the bridges had persistent technical challenges. After a few years, it stopped using them in Texas. But in Albany, where the airport owned the bridges, they remained in use until 2019. In 2018, Southwest began testing dual boarding again in Sacramento and San Jose, California—with old-fashioned open-air stairs rather than the custom jet bridges at the rear of the plane. To this day, Southwest continues to study ways to improve the process.

Not all of the Company's enhancements were by choice. With the stricter government security measures adopted after 9/11, Southwest retired the plastic passes and replaced them with paper ones that were printed with a Customer's name, date, flight number, confirmation number, and departure and arrival information.

Over the years, countless studies have shown that Southwest can get Customers on a plane more quickly by letting them choose their own seats. In fact, its tests have shown that assigned seating can even increase boarding time by as much as four minutes. Faster boarding means better ontime performance and cost savings that help keep ticket prices low.

But even some of the Company's most devoted Customers have a love-hate relationship with the ever-efficient open seating practice. They love Southwest's low fares, but they often don't like finding themselves in the last boarding group or in a middle seat. Many have developed their own seating strategies, and Customers who fly more can qualify for A-List or A-List Preferred boarding positions.

Travel columnists and bloggers have written dozens of articles about how to get the best seats on Southwest flights.

After the Company introduced EarlyBird Check-In®, a game theorist even weighed in with his analysis.

(Southwest didn't actually use game theory in offering Customers the opportunity to pay a little more to reserve a spot in the first boarding group, but, hey, if he thinks the Company is pretty smart, who's to argue?) For Southwest, it's still simply the most efficient way to get people on a plane.

By the early 2000s, many people assumed that Customers were tiring of open seating and would prefer an assigned seat. Southwest tried assigning seats on 200 flights out of San Diego and conducted a similar test in San Antonio. It surveyed Customers and Rapid Rewards® Members, and the results were clear: Customers liked having the freedom to choose where they sit.

Southwest did, however, find some changes to make. While open seating remained, the Company said goodbye to first-come, first-served boarding. Instead of Customers rushing to get to the gate early in hopes of securing their favorite window or aisle seat, Southwest began assigning Customers a number and a boarding group based on when they check in for a flight. At the gate, Customers find the steel stanchion—designed internally at Southwest—that corresponds with their boarding number, and Operations Agents call enplaning Customers to board in numerical order within their assigned group.

Once they're on the plane, though, it still works like it does at church—you can sit anywhere you want.

Rapid Rewards
SOUTHWEST AIRLINES
0000 123456789 0
EXPIRATION DATE
12/98
MEMBER SINCE
06/87
HERB KELLEHER

Reaping Rewards (Rapidly)

From its first Frequent Flyer program, the Company Club, to today's Rapid Rewards®, Southwest has made it easy for Members to benefit from their loyalty.

In 1986, a young, mustachioed, guitar-playing accountant named Gary Kelly joined Southwest as Controller. As a much smaller Company back then, its focus had been on the frontlines—serving the Customer, adding aircraft. The back office, where Gary found himself, was "kind of a mess" and lacked many of the capabilities to put the Company's great ideas into action.

The most glaring omission: "The Company didn't have computers for all the back office functions," recalled Gary, who would later become Chief Financial Officer and eventually Chairman, President, and CEO. Gary set about trying to build financial systems and other back-office basics, when, later in 1986, a new assignment came down: Southwest needed a Frequent Flyer program.

Its old rival, Texas International, created the first true mileage-based frequent flyer program in 1979.

Southwest faced mounting pressure from its Customers to create one. Not surprisingly, Herb resisted.

"Herb was so cost-conscious because he knew that our cost advantage was our ultimate lever against our competition, because we could charge such prices they couldn't match," said Dave Ridley, retired Senior Vice President Business Development.

In true Southwest fashion, Gary and the Team got the whole program off the ground in record time.

"I became a Leader on that project, and in 90 days we had a computer system, we had a process, and we got it out the door," Gary said. "I was really proud of that. We were small but nimble, as Herb would always say, and it was a great learning experience."

The Company Club, as the program was known, debuted in 1987. As the name implies, it was geared toward business travelers who were the most frequent Customers on Southwest's short-haul routes. The Company Club awarded free tickets based on the total trips flown, regardless of distance. Because most other airlines awarded tickets based on miles flown, the Company Club gave Members a chance to earn rewards faster than they could with competitors' programs.

Once again, Southwest chose a simple approach that, today, is used more often to earn a free sandwich at your favorite deli than for air travel.

Because it wasn't tracking miles, Members who had flown 20 one-way flights got a pass stamped at check-in for each additional flight. After collecting 16

stamps (the equivalent of eight round trips) in a year or less, Members earned a round trip award ticket.

One of the most popular bonuses to the program was—and still is—coupons for free premium drinks, including alcoholic beverages. (Southwest offers complimentary nonalcoholic refreshments onboard all flights.)

←
Gary—minus a phone booth—unveils the details of the new Rapid Rewards program in January 2011.

↓
The Rapid Rewards Credit Card offers Members the ability to earn points—even while they're on the ground.

Southwest also created the Companion Pass, which quickly became the top benefit of the program—and remains so. Members who fly 100 qualifying one-way flights (or earn 125,000 qualifying points by using the Southwest Airlines Rapid Rewards® Credit Card from Chase) in a calendar year receive a pass to designate a companion to travel with them, when a seat is available, for just the cost of the government-imposed fees and taxes. The program is frequently touted on travel blogs as a top perk because even if a Companion Pass Member is using an award ticket, the Companion can still fly with them for free (plus the taxes and fees). As one travel blogger noted, earning a Companion Pass effectively doubles the value of a Passenger's points.

In 1996, the Company relaunched The Company Club as Rapid Rewards®, but the awards didn't change—a round trip award ticket after eight round trip flights.

The Company Club and Rapid Rewards were designed with short-haul flights in mind, but by 2011, Southwest was flying more long-haul service. So, it revamped Rapid Rewards, removing blackout dates to allow Members to redeem points for any flight on any day. And rather than awarding travel by trip segment, it adjusted the formula to award points based on every dollar Members spend for their own travel on Southwest.

Over the years, Rapid Rewards has contributed significantly to Southwest's profits and was an important driver of the Company's growth in the 2010s. In October 2019, Southwest added a new benefit: Rapid Rewards Points would no longer expire, even if not used during a 24-month period.

Rapid Rewards has come a long way since Southwest's first computers, but the Company continues to reevaluate the benefits, adding new Partners and services as a way of saying "thank you" to its Customers.

Oozing Authenticity Online

In June 2006, Gary Kelly, then Southwest's CEO and Vice Chairman, sat down at his computer and started writing. "I'm new to this whole blogosphere thing. ..."

Actually, almost everyone was. Southwest had started a Company blog, *Nuts About Southwest*, just two months earlier. At the time, few Fortune 500 companies were blogging, and Southwest was the first airline to open an online dialog with its Customers.

Gary decided to test the waters of the blogosphere by wading into a controversial topic: Southwest's open-seating policy. He followed up on some comments he'd made in his annual address to Shareholders a month earlier. He noted that although open seating had been very effective for the Company, it was evaluating the possibility of assigning seats.

Southwest started blogging in 2006 and now connects with Customers 24/7 on social media with the help of its state-of-the-art Listening Center.

Twitter Trends (Today)
Hank Aaron
293K
247K
Volume of Social Conversation (Last 7 Days)
SOUTHWEST
DELTA
AMERICAN
JETBLUE
UNITED
rapid
opens
dates
social
numbers
high
travel
change
work
reservation
picks
Share of Voice (Today)
45%
22%

Gary—and everyone else at Southwest—quickly learned the power of the blogosphere. The post was met with about 700 comments (truly significant in the early days of blogging), about 80 percent of which urged the Company to keep things as they were.

"Honestly, we had no idea how much our loyal Customers loved our open-seating policy until they started telling us on our blog," Colleen, who was President at the time, said a year later.

"One thing's for sure, if we do decide to stay with it, we'll never apologize for it again!"

When Southwest unveiled its blog in 2006, it had a simple goal: "to give our readers the opportunity to take a look inside Southwest Airlines and to interact with us."

Initially, the blog had 30 Employees, including Mechanics, Customer Service Agents, Flight Attendants, Pilots, Marketers, Schedule Planners, and more who agreed to participate by providing content.

"Blogging works for us because, as a Company, we know we have nothing to hide," Colleen said. "Our Employees absolutely ooze authenticity, and our bloggers have been able to bring that same spirit to the blog."

In the first year, the Company published 265 blog posts and generated more than 6,300 comments, including the 700 that responded to Gary. Over the years, it has continued to pioneer the corporate use of social media, and it's been recognized for embracing social technologies.

In 2014, Southwest opened its state-of-the-art Listening Center at Headquarters. Employees monitor comments from Customers via Southwest's social media platforms around the clock and provide real-time feedback, which is disseminated across the organization to improve operations and Customer Service. It's become part of a vital system of two-way communication with Customers.

The Listening Center also works closely with Network Operations Control (NOC). A satellite Listening Center within the NOC relays real-time operational updates to Customers as they become available.

That came in handy on October 11, 2015, when a technical glitch grounded some 800 Southwest flights, causing delays for thousands of Customers. The Company received a lot of angry tweets and comments on various social media platforms from Customers who were stranded in long lines. It kept everyone updated as information became available, and it responded to each of the tens of thousands of posts and tweets. The experience in using social media to communicate with Customers proved to be crucial a year later, when a computer failure disrupted Southwest's operations for three days, affecting thousands of flights. Because Company email was also affected, social media was the only way Southwest Employees could communicate with Customers.

During the COVID-19 pandemic, Southwest used social media to encourage Customers to join the airline in its #SouthwestHeartStrong campaign supporting nonprofits bringing lifesaving materials to communities affected by the pandemic.

Of course, Southwest also uses social media to have some fun, such as its #FeesDontFly campaign. The Company used the hashtag to reward people who were expressing displeasure with the hidden fees charged by some competitors, offering them Southwest® gift cards, or, in some cases, tickets on Southwest. It also found ways to surprise, delight, and reward its most active followers.

These days, Southwest gets as many as 3,000 inbound posts a day on Twitter and Facebook, and its 40 Listening Center Employees respond to every one as quickly as possible. The Company is no longer a newbie in the blogosphere—or on social media, for that matter—but it continues to look for new ways to use online technology to connect with its Customers.

↓
Listening Center Employees collaborate on how to best serve their Customers via social media.

Bagging the Fees

By 2007, the airline industry was beginning to see signs of a significant recession that would prove to be one of the most challenging periods in commercial aviation history.

Oil prices rose heading into the summer of 2008, hitting a record $147 a barrel. Southwest had a strong financial position, but many of its competitors were struggling. In a play for revenue, other airlines began imposing fees for traditional services, such as the first two checked bags or making a change to a ticket.

Southwest refused. It always believed in a "what-you-see-is-what-you-get" approach with Customers, which it later advertised as a "no hidden fees" policy.

"We said, 'We're not going to do that,'" Chairman and CEO Gary Kelly recalled. "There were a lot of naysayers saying, 'No, you've got to—earnings aren't where they need to be. There's a revenue gap here.'"

Other airlines may charge passengers for checked baggage, but at Southwest, the first two checked bags—within weight and size limits, of course—fly free.

Nonstop Love
is finally here.
Southwest
Southwest
One Team. All Heart.

But to Gary and other Southwest Leaders, charging for the first two checked bags was a short-term gain that risked alienating long-term Customers.

"It takes five or six bags, in terms of charges, to offset the loss of just one Customer," Gary said.

Competitors started adding new fees—fees for aisle seating, fees for meals, and even fees for carry-on bags. And one airline elsewhere in the world even suggested (without following through) that it might charge passengers for using the lavatory.

"We are convinced that not charging for the first two checked bags within weight and size limits wins us more Customers, and therefore more revenue and more profits, as compared to doing what everybody else does, which Customers universally hate," Gary said. "Charging for the first two checked bags goes against everything we stand for."

Instead of charging for the first two checked bags like many competitors, Southwest returned to its tried-and-true battle plan. Employees pulled together and developed initiatives to differentiate Southwest even more from its competitors and make its operations even more efficient.

In 2010, the Company took a stand. It outfitted 50 aircraft with the slogan "Free Bags Fly Here" and an arrow pointing to the plane's cargo hold. Then it tagged about 1,000 Cargo Carts across its system with banners that said, "I Carry Free Bags."

Those efforts, combined with other behind-the-scenes measures—such as strategically trimming flight schedules and rotating aircraft into key airports—helped Southwest boost its profitability without yielding to the fee pressure.

"I'm proud of that, in retrospect," Gary said. "By the time we got to 2009, which was a really difficult year, we were well outperforming the industry in terms of our revenue production."

More than a decade after bags fly free® was introduced, it has become as much a part of the Company's brand today as peanuts and hot pants were in the 1970s.

"It just turned out to be wildly successful for us," Gary said. "A lot of good things were happening to lay the groundwork for committing to an even bolder strategy." That strategy would ultimately become known as Trans**fare**ncy®.

"And 'bags fly free,'" Gary said, "was a key step."

➔
After introducing what became one of its most successful promotions, Southwest used luggage carts to advertise the Company's position on checked baggage.

FREE BAGS FLY HERE
I CARRY FREE BAGS.
Weight and size limits apply.

Transfarency®

[Trans-fair-uhn-see] ***n.***

1. Philosophy created by Southwest Airlines in which Customers are treated honestly and fairly, and how fares actually stay low.

Freedom from Fee-dom

When it comes to fees, Southwest has nothing to hide and even coined a term to describe its position: Trans**fare**ncy®.

The bags fly free® campaign had shown that Customers appreciated Southwest's approach to avoiding the fees that, by 2015, had become the industry norm. That year, the Company launched an all-out assault on hidden fees with a campaign called Trans**fare**ncy®. It was designed to reinforce everything that makes Southwest different from other carriers. Quite simply, "Trans**fare**ncy" meant that its low fares weren't hiding anything—no bag fees for the first and second checked bags within certain weight and size limits, no fees for changing a reservation (although there could be a fare difference), and no hidden charges.

The Trans**fare**ncy campaign used the hashtag #FeesDontFly, and it became an instant hit with Customers. Southwest kicked off the campaign with a television ad and shared it on the Company's social medial channels, racking up 5 million likes on Facebook.

As part of the campaign, Southwest unveiled a website, Trans**fare**ncy.com, that compared the Company's fee structure with those of competitors. It offered interactive games, including "Fee or Fake," which challenged visitors to distinguish real fees charged by competitors from fake ones. (It was harder than it seemed.)

The site also collected cheeky suggestions from Customers about how to save on fees, such as wearing their entire wardrobe to avoid checking luggage or shipping their clothes to their destination ahead of their trip. Participants who submitted the most creative ideas received a Southwest® gift card as a surprise and delight.

While Southwest had fun at its rivals' expense, many of the other carriers still didn't get it. By 2019, Southwest was the only major airline to offer bags fly free® to everyone.* In 2019 alone, more than 97 million bags flew free on Southwest, and as CEO Gary Kelly put it, "We would rather have the Customers than the bag fees." Southwest estimated that it gained a one-point boost in domestic market share over several years following the implementation of industry bag fees as a result of additional Customers from not charging for the first two checked bags, which was more than the Company estimated it could have generated by following suit with the industry.

In fact, the industry loved fees so much that Wall Street analysts came up with a fancy name for them—"ancillary revenue." (Southwest does offer additional products for purchase.)

Regardless of what Wall Street called them, Southwest knew the fees meant added costs for Customers, and it refused to go along with the trend. It even ran ads highlighting how much its Customers saved.

Southwest coined the term "Trans**fare**ncy" to include more than just the lack of hidden fees. It was a whole marketing initiative that coincided with the 2015 launch of a new international terminal at Houston (Hobby) and included a preview of the Company's new Heart cabin that was rolled out in 2016. The Company also launched supporting advertising campaigns, such as "Yes!," in the fall of 2016. "Yes!" used Employees in music video situations at the airport. In the videos, a Customer would ask if Southwest could fly to a certain destination, or provide a certain service without a fee, and the Employees would break into song, singing "Yes!" The campaign slogan was "In a world full of no, we're a plane full of yes."

The ads also helped promote new international destinations: "Say 'Yes' to low fares and faraway destinations."

Trans*fare*ncy followed Southwest's long history of democratizing the skies and treating Customers with honesty and respect.

It showed how the Company connects Customers with the people and things they care about most. That's been at the Heart of everything Southwest has done since it started flying. There's nothing ancillary about it.

(**First and second checked pieces of luggage; weight and size limits apply; some carriers offer free checked bags on select routes or in qualified circumstances.*)

→
A 2015 jetway poster compares the differences between Southwest and the competition.

'Unmatchable'

The recession of the early 1990s was a challenging time for the commercial airline industry. With Iraq's invasion of Kuwait and then Operation Desert Storm, fuel prices rose sharply, and bookings slowed, threatening Southwest's growth plans at a critical time.

"In addition to recession, which dampens travel demand, there was the fear of terrorism, so it was a rough time, and we lost money in the fourth quarter of '90," said Gary Kelly, then Chief Financial Officer. "It was a really rough time."

Desperate to get Customers in its seats, Southwest began a promotional campaign in May 1991 known as "Kids Fly Free." Two months later, it expanded the campaign to "Friends Fly Free," which essentially offered two tickets for the price of one unrestricted fare. Any adult, 18 years or older, could travel with a friend of any age without paying for a second ticket.

A critical promotion at a critical time, "Friends Fly Free" became one of the greatest competitive moves in airline history.

BEST
FRIENDS

THIS SUMMER

KIDS FLY FREE.

NO ADVANCE PURCHASE AND FULLY REFUNDABLE.

Great news for summer vacation budgets. Kids Fly Free on Southwest Airlines. Here's how:

- Just buy a ticket at our regular low unrestricted fare, and your young companion will get another ticket on the same flight free.
- The offer is good only for a child 17 years or younger traveling with someone 18 or older. Proof of age is required. One child per adult.
- Make reservations at least one day before travel and fly from May 22 through September 8, 1992.
- Call **1-800-I-FLY-SWA** (1-800-435-9792) or your travel agent soon. Seats are limited and won't be available on some flights during peak times. Fun Fares,* Senior, Youth, Military, and other promotional fares or offers do not apply.

Fly Southwest Airlines and save on your family travel all summer. It's Just Plane Smart.

SOUTHWEST AIRLINES

Just Plane Smart.

AND REMEMBER, FRIENDS CAN STILL FLY FREE THROUGH MAY 21ST

FRIENDS FLY FREE THIS SUMMER.

ONLY SOUTHWEST AIRLINES LETS YOU BRING ALONG A FRIEND FREE ON ANY OF OUR FLIGHTS.

Just buy a roundtrip ticket at our regular low unrestricted fare, and your traveling companion will get another roundtrip ticket on the same flight free.

Take advantage of this great offer. Just call your travel agent or call us at 1-800-I-FLY-SWA (1-800-435-9792). It's Just Plane Smart.

FREE TO BRING A FRIEND ALONG FOR FREE.

For our Friends Fly Free offer, you must be an adult, age 18 or older. The friend you bring along for free may be any age.

FREE FROM ADVANCE PURCHASE.

Your roundtrip travel must take place by September 8, 1992. Make roundtrip reservations at least one day before departure. You and your travel partner must travel together on the same flights, and your plans must include a stayover of one night or longer.

FREE OF PENALTIES. FULLY REFUNDABLE.

Tickets are fully refundable without penalty. Seats for these offers are limited and won't be available on some flights that operate during peak travel times. Fun Fares,® Senior, Youth, Military, and other promotional fares or offers do not apply.

SOUTHWEST AIRLINES℠

Just Plane Smart.℠

1-800-I-FLY-SWA
(1-800-435-9792)

"We came up with the Friends Fly Free campaign, which blew the doors off," said Dave Ridley, who was a Director in Marketing at the time. "That really catapulted our business in the fall of '91, continued in '92, and we were still running Friends Fly Free in 1995."

What had started as a temporary promotion to get the Company through the recession proved so popular that Southwest continued it for five years.

Friends Fly Free was a critical promotion at a critical time. Herb saw the promotion and others like it as essential to Southwest's survival, because the airline business is primarily one of fixed costs. This was even more true for Southwest, which, unlike its competitors, prioritized protecting Employees and preserving job security during difficult economic times.

"We are basically going to pay the same People costs; pay the same operating costs; pay the same aircraft ownership costs, and operate the same number of flights in bad times, as well as in good times," he said in the fall of 1991.

"How well we do financially is determined not by the fare that an individual Customer pays but by the total revenue that a given flight generates."

The 1991 "Kids Fly Free" promotion allowed anyone under age 18 to fly free when accompanied by an adult paying the regular unrestricted fare.

Rather than fly a plane with empty seats, it made more financial sense to fill those remaining seats at lower fares, Herb argued.

"Without promotions like 'Friends Fly Free', our 1991 load factors would have been embarrassing, our gross revenues substantially reduced, and our profits radically impaired," he said.

In fact, Friends Fly Free was so effective, Southwest revived it in 1997 and 1998, and again in 2002.

Competitors tried to match the promotion, but other airlines' two-for-one sales lasted only a short time.

"We could let someone come on and fly free and still make money," Dave said. "It was unmatchable."

Disrupting the Industry

Bucking Tradition and Blazing a Trail

Southwest

GOT YOUR COMPANY
CLUB CREDIT?

BOARDING
PASS

THIS IS NOT A TICKET

THIS PASS ENTITLES
THE HOLDER TO BOARD
THE AIRCRAFT. IT IS
THE PROPERTY OF
SOUTHWEST AIRLINES
AND MUST BE
SURRENDERED UPO

SOUTHWEST

Grow West, Young Airline

The famous plastic boarding passes took on an unusual shape for Southwest's entry into the California market.

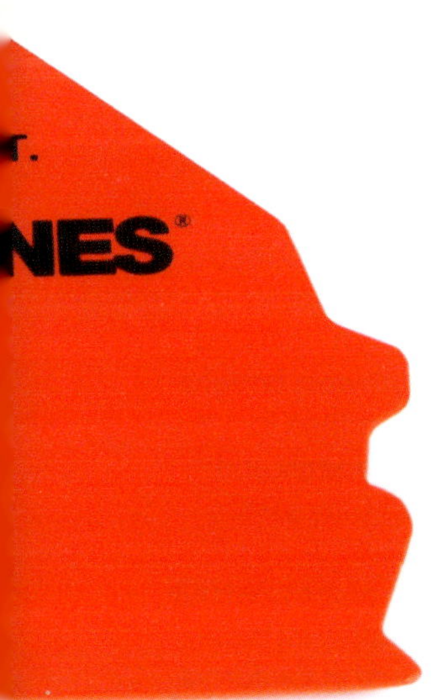

By 1982, most of Southwest's flights were in Texas, New Mexico, Oklahoma, and Louisiana. However, with the Wright Amendment restricting long-haul flights from Dallas, the Company began looking at other airports for expansion. Increasingly, its gaze turned westward.

Southwest added service to Phoenix and Las Vegas and set its sights on California. The airline got a foothold in San Diego with six flights a day, but gates and route approvals for markets such as Los Angeles and San Francisco were hard to come by due to the air traffic controllers' strike in 1981. The Civil Aeronautics Board (CAB), however, held some routes in reserve for "new entrants."

That gave Founder Herb Kelleher an idea. Southwest wasn't a new entrant, of course; it had already been flying for more than a decade. But a few years earlier, when Lamar Muse was still President and CEO, he'd proposed starting a separate airline at Chicago (Midway). Southwest's Board of Directors didn't adopt the plan, but during the consideration process, the Company had incorporated a subsidiary, Midway Southwest. It existed only on paper—it never operated or owned a single plane. Herb identified this paper subsidiary as a new entrant, applied for routes, and then traded them to the "real" Southwest.

The CAB wasn't amused and nullified the deal, ruling that routes could be transferred only to an operating airline. So Herb sold Midway Southwest to a charter company that had a single Learjet. The charter operator acquired the routes and traded them to Southwest. (The CAB administrator, while not openly approving of what Herb had done, was privately impressed by his ingenuity.) Herb had found a back door into Los Angeles, and in September 1982, Southwest initiated service with three flights a day. A month later, it added four daily flights to San Francisco. By the time the year ended, it added six new Western cities to its network. And it wasn't done.

California was a critical market, and a decade after Southwest started flying there, the Company found itself in an intense battle with other carriers that actually thought they could beat it at the low-fare game.

"We put our chips on California, and these big airlines were taking a little subset of their fleet and trying to offer a lower fare, make them no frills, and trying to compete directly with Southwest Airlines, because we were winning California," said retired Executive Vice President Daily Operations Greg Wells, who joined the Company in 1981 as a Ramp Agent at Houston (Hobby) and Dallas (Love Field) and later became a Station Manager in Phoenix and then San Jose. "And we did win. And we're still winning in California."

Greg recalls one aspect of the California expansion that didn't go quite so smoothly. By the 1980s, Southwest was using plastic boarding passes, which were normally rectangular.

"We thought it would be clever to get a boarding pass shaped like the state of California," Greg recalled.

"It looked really neat. Try being an Ops Agent, yanking those things, and stacking them." The irregular shape not only made them hard to stack and organize, they frequently slipped out of agents' hands and spilled on the floor. One industrious Employee even took the initiative to build wooden holders specially designed to contain the irregularly shaped boarding passes.

Southwest's westward expansion plans called for the addition of 21 new jets. Herb's aversion to debt, however, led to a Companywide austerity program so it could pay cash for the new planes. And that's what it did.

The Company further strengthened its position in California in the early 1990s. With the Iraqi invasion of Kuwait in 1990, oil prices soared, and the U.S. economy went into a recession. USAir had bought Pacific Southwest Airlines (PSA)—the carrier Southwest had used as a template for its business model—but in 1991, USAir pulled out of the state.

"We were stunned," Chairman and CEO Gary Kelly recalled. "We would have paid good money for access to some of those cities." As it was, Southwest ordered more aircraft to take over some of the old PSA routes and gates, which were suddenly available. Not long after that, American acquired AirCal, which operated 737s that American didn't want, so Southwest bought six of its planes. And when America West filed for bankruptcy and shrunk significantly in Phoenix and Las Vegas, "We rushed in more flights," Gary said.

Because of its strong balance sheet, an aggressive but strategic growth plan, and true grit, Southwest was able to significantly increase its presence in California at a time when most of its competitors were struggling. And that, pardners, is how "the West was won."

↑
Among Southwest's special liveries is *California One*, a 737-700 honoring the Golden State. Southwest began serving California in 1982 with service to San Diego, the Company's 18th destination.

The Battle for Midway

Herb, decked out in a green sport coat and hat, ushered in service at Chicago's Midway Airport on St. Patrick's Day, 1985.

Southwest had been eyeing Chicago's Midway Airport as far back as 1976, before deregulation, when the Civil Aeronautics Board (CAB) began floating the concept of low-fare service in key markets. That gave Lamar Muse, President and CEO at the time, an idea.

Midway was similar to Dallas Love Field—close to the downtown area of a major city and underserved by other carriers. As Lamar saw it, convincing the CAB to let Southwest operate from Midway would bring low fares to the Midwest and meet the Company's own growth needs into the 1980s.

Word of his plans got out, however, and soon paperwork had been filed by someone else to create a new carrier called Midway Airlines, which filed an application for service in August 1976. Lamar presented his Chicago plan to Southwest's Board of Directors, urging them to incorporate a Chicago subsidiary as well. That company, Midway (Southwest) Airway Co., was formed on paper—later playing a key role in Southwest's entry into California—but the Board ultimately rejected the idea to start service in Chicago. Southwest's Directors felt the move would have required a rapid surge in growth, adding a fleet of new planes and Employees at a rate that was simply too much too fast.

But Southwest never completely took its eyes off Midway. In 1985, its westward expansion shifted northward, with the addition of eight nonstop flights from Midway. The Company initiated service on St. Patrick's Day, ushered in by more than 100 Employees arriving on the first flight, led by Southwest Founder Herb Kelleher, wearing a green sport coat, green bowler hat, and a pin that read "Irish Power." The transplanted Texas leprechauns took to the streets and marched in the city's annual St. Patrick's Day parade. Five years later, the Company was operating 43 flights a day from four gates. Very quickly, it needed more space. Getting it was easier said than done.

Southwest flew a Team, including lead negotiator and then-Vice President Government Affairs Ron Ricks, to Chicago to convince city leaders to give Southwest more gates. They quickly told Ron that Midway Airlines was the hometown carrier, and Southwest wouldn't be adding any more flights as long as Midway Airlines was around.

"I'm just going to tell you that this is a horse race, and you just bet on the wrong horse," Ron told the city representatives.

"When Midway Airlines fails, and you've got 20 unused gates, and the airport is now losing money, you just give us a call and we'll help you out."

Four months later that's exactly what happened. In March 1991, Midway Airlines filed for bankruptcy. Herb went to the bankruptcy court and offered to make payments that would keep Midway in business in exchange for Southwest receiving more gates.

Northwest Airlines, however, had other ideas. Even though it didn't operate at Midway, it showed up in court and promised to hire all the Midway Airlines employees. Herb refused to make such an offer, because it wasn't realistic. (He did agree to interview Midway Airlines employees and give them priority consideration for future positions.) The judge ruled in Northwest's favor, giving it all the gates.

A few weeks later, however, Northwest realized it had overpromised, and on November 13, 1991, it backed out of its plan to buy Midway Airlines.

The mayor of Chicago, who had been eager to expand Midway Airport, called Herb. The conversation was short and sweet:

"You want gates?"

"Yes," Herb replied.

"How many do you want?"

"All of them," Herb said.

But it wouldn't be that easy. After all, Northwest had already bought the gates. Jim Parker, who was then Vice President General Counsel, found a solution. He scoured the terms of the airport agreement and found that the city could let another airline occupy the Midway Airlines gates if they were not being used by their primary tenant. With Midway Airlines on the brink of ceasing operations, the city could award Southwest the gates.

Southwest's Leaders had already drawn up plans for "Operation Midway," and they wasted no time acting on them. On November 14—one day after Northwest backed out of its plan to buy Midway Airlines—Southwest shipped computers, signs, and other equipment needed to take over the gates. Southwest also pledged $20 million to develop and promote the airport, and it committed to explore further expansion.

Southwest's move into Midway became "a launching-off point for service to New York ... to Detroit and to the West Coast," said John Denison, Executive Vice President Corporate Services at the time, who was involved in some of the Midway negotiations. "[It gave] us a whole different access point."

Fast-forward to 2004; Southwest seized an opportunity to acquire the assets of ATA Airlines, which operated six gates at Midway, thus boosting Southwest's capacity there by 32 percent. (ATA continued to operate as a separate carrier until April 2008.)

As of mid-2020, Southwest was operating 32 gates at Midway, and the economic impact of its operations was estimated to be about $8 billion annually.

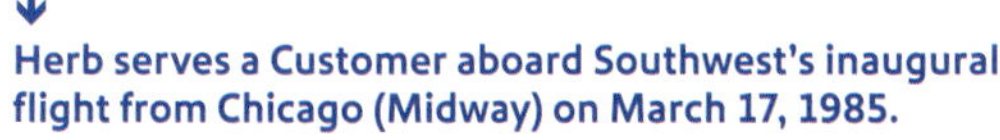

Herb serves a Customer aboard Southwest's inaugural flight from Chicago (Midway) on March 17, 1985.

Southwest
Southwest.com

Flying Flags and Flying Fish*

A bit of *plane* marketing genius spawned a host of iconic Southwest liveries.

Something was going on in a Boeing hangar in Seattle on May 17, 1988, but only a handful of people knew what was happening. Given the code name "Project Friend," the production schedule for a new 737 had been changed to complete flight tests before the plane was painted.

Then, for the next two days, the painting of the jet progressed under the supervision of what may have been the most unlikely pairing in the history of airplane liveries: Tim McClure, chief creative officer for the Austin advertising firm GSD&M, and a SeaWorld zoologist.

Over the next couple of days, workers applied 96 gallons of paint, 18 of them the typical Southwest desert gold, orange, and red. But the project also required 48 gallons of white gloss and 30 gallons of black.

What emerged from the hangar around midnight on May 22 was unlike anything the airline industry—or the world of marine biology—had ever seen. In the dead of night, it was flown from Seattle to a remote airfield in Houston; then on the morning of May 23, it arrived in San Antonio.

An astonished crowd looked on as what appeared to be a giant flying killer whale descended from the skies. Once on the ground, it was greeted by Herb and the mayor of San Antonio, dressed in tuxedos, or "penguin suits." Also in the crowd was the chairman of SeaWorld of Texas, a $170 million, 416-acre water and marine park that was about to become the city's biggest tourist attraction after the Alamo.

Christened *Shamu One*, after SeaWorld's famous whale, the plane went on a 27-city tour around Southwest's network, and even made a special trip to New York (LaGuardia), where the airline didn't fly at the time, to pick up travel writers and bring them to San Antonio for SeaWorld's grand opening. The "whale of a promotion" drew headlines in newspapers from Lubbock to San Francisco, as well as national publications such as *USA Today* and *Time* magazine.

↑
***Shamu One*, the result of a unique partnership between Southwest and SeaWorld of Texas, took to the skies on May 23, 1988.**

Tim had concocted the cross-marketing idea. GSD&M was Southwest's ad agency, and the firm hoped to land the SeaWorld account. He had painted a model of a 737 with the killer whale design himself, leaving only the familiar "Southwest" lettering and tail colors from the airline's traditional livery. He asked Colleen if he needed Herb's blessing to pitch the deal. "No," Colleen said. "Go pitch it to SeaWorld. If they like it, he'll like it."

When Tim pulled back the covering on the model he'd made, a collective gasp arose from the SeaWorld representatives.

Their only question was whether such a stunning cross-promotion was possible. They didn't yet know Herb or Southwest. Herb, of course, loved the whole idea. Southwest worked out the painting details with Boeing to keep the project under wraps, and SeaWorld's head zoologist made sure the paint scheme was accurate.

Southwest not only continued to fly *Shamu One* in its regular flight schedule, it also offered bumper stickers to every Customer who boarded the plane and held three months' worth of inflight contests in which one winner per flight won free tickets to SeaWorld.

SeaWorld, in turn, made Southwest its official airline and painted the Southwest name and colors on the Sky Tower at its San Diego park, one of the most visible attractions. *Shamu One* proved so popular that, by the fall of 1990, Southwest had three Shamu planes. The Shamu fleet flew until 2014, when the two companies decided to end their partnership after their contract expired.

The SeaWorld partnership, however, touched off a new era of specialty liveries. In the past, the Company had dedicated planes to Original Employees, and it had designated the first 737-300 in 1984 as *The Spirit of Kitty Hawk*, in honor of the Wright brothers on the 81st anniversary of their historic flight. But now, it began repainting fuselages to recognize Company milestones and honor states in which it operated. In 1990, it rolled out *Lone Star One*, with the fuselage wrapped in a stylized version of the Texas flag to honor its home state. Over the next 29 years, the Company added 11 more similar state tributes, from California to Maryland.

In 1996, it launched *Silver One*, with an unpainted, shiny fuselage, in honor of the Company's 25th anniversary. A year later, it debuted *Triple Crown One*, which included the names of all 24,000 Employees at the time on the overhead bins, in recognition of having the best ontime performance, fewest mishandled bags, and fewest customer complaints of any major airline for five years in a row. (Southwest awarded itself the Triple Crown, a self-proclaimed honor, based on statistics compiled by the Department of Transportation.)

The SeaWorld promotion, and all the later special liveries it inspired, helped project Southwest's Fun-LUVing image onto its aircraft, but it also did something no one thought possible. It proved a whale could fly.

*(*Yes, Shamu is actually a mammal, but "Flying Water-Dwelling Mammal" doesn't have the same ring to it.)*

↑
During the Company's 50th anniversary celebration at the Houston (Hobby) Technical Operations Hangar on June 18, 2021, Gary Kelly unveiled *Freedom One*, a high-flying tribute to 50 years of Southwest Airlines service with a symbol of unwavering pride for the nation and its heroes.

T.J. LUV Says 'I Do'

After years of being single, Southwest's mascot T.J. LUV finally got hitched in February 1994. T.J., which the Company adopted in 1983, was wed to Morris Magic, the mascot of Morris Air, at the Graceland Wedding Chapel in Las Vegas.

After a rendition of a popular Las Vegas "anthem" and with T.J. waiting at the altar, everyone turned to watch the blushing bride taxi down the aisle. The two joined wings as they exchanged vows.

"In turbulence and clear skies, may your magic never mellow and may your spirit always soar," the "officiant" (impersonating a beloved rock 'n' roll icon) declared, noting that the union had been blessed by the FAA, DOT, and the Department of Justice. Then, he pronounced the couple cleared to fly.

T.J. LUV's "marriage" to Morris Magic was cute and fun, and celebrated a merging of "kindred spirits." For Southwest, it proved to be a strategic acquisition.

MORRIS AIRBEAR

DEPARTMENT
OF
JUSTICE

As the newlyweds departed, Flight Attendants and Pilots from both companies showered the happy couple with bags of peanuts, and Morris Magic threw her bouquet of peanut packets into the crowd.

The nuptials celebrated Southwest's acquisition, completed at the end of 1993, when it bought Salt Lake City-based Morris Air in a stock swap worth $129 million. June Morris had founded the company as a travel agency while working from her husband's photo shop and built it into the largest in Utah. In 1984, she parlayed her travel agency success into a charter airline, Morris Air, and, in 1992, it began scheduled service with a fleet of 21 Boeing 737s. When the company approached Southwest a year later about a merger, Southwest jumped at the chance. June had modeled her company after Southwest, which is part of the reason Herb declared, "We are kindred spirits."

With few overlapping routes, the acquisition gave Southwest a critical foothold in the Northwest.

The financial community declared the Morris acquisition "one of the most positive, one of the most beneficial transactions in the history of Southwest Airlines," Herb said in his 1994 Message to the Field.

←
T.J. LUV and Morris Magic took a charter trip down the aisle at the Graceland Wedding Chapel in Las Vegas to symbolically seal the acquisition of Morris Air in February 1994.

Not only did Morris have a fleet of compatible aircraft, it was also a young company that hadn't yet developed "bad habits." Also, it didn't have any unions, which made workforce integration easier.

While Southwest wasn't a small Company anymore, it still thought it was. When it submitted the merger information for the U.S. Department of Justice's antitrust review, investigators were surprised that it was less than an inch thick. They told Herb he might have forgotten something. "Well, we're not very big on documents at Southwest Airlines," Herb replied. Of course, the department found everything in order and approved the merger.

After the transaction closed on December 31, 1993, June joined Southwest's Board of Directors and served until 2006. The Morris acquisition enabled the Company to add an unprecedented seven cities in 1994, and by quickly adding new planes to its fleet, Southwest was able to beef up on key markets in the West that were about to come under fire from yet another attempt by its biggest rivals to stop the Company's growth.

Cumulative Effect of LUV

Southwest always knew it had a positive effect on the communities it serves. It doesn't look at new destinations in terms of how many people are already flying there, but by how many more would fly if it was easy and affordable. As the Company grew, it learned that when people discovered its low fares, more of them started coming aboard.

In 1993, the U.S. Department of Transportation (DOT) confirmed the phenomena. It released a study showing that whenever Southwest began serving a new city, average fares decreased, and the number of passengers increased.

"Most of the markets involve other airlines' hub city, sometimes two hub cities, yet Southwest dominates market share virtually every where [sic] it serves," the report found. It went on to quantify that dominance: Southwest's average share of its top 100 markets was 65 percent, compared with less than 40 percent for other carriers. And Southwest had a 50 percent or greater market share in 80 of those markets. "No other airline comes close to these numbers ... and Southwest's dominance is almost universally pervasive."

For years, the "Southwest Effect" has been behind lowered fares and increased traffic in cities across the Company's route map.

Go See Do
Places.
People.
Things.
Southwest
pacific
mountain
central
Seattle
Portland
Spokane
Sacramento
Oakland
San Francisco
Boise
San Jose
Reno/Tahoe
Los Angeles (LAX)
Burbank
Orange County
Ontario
Las Vegas
Salt Lake City
San Diego
Indianapolis, Phoenix, and Tucson do not observe Daylight Saving Time.
Phoenix
Tucson
Albuquerque
El Paso
Amarillo
Lubbock
Midland/ Odessa
San Antonio
Austin
Chicago (Midway)
St. Louis
Little Rock
Turn your phone bil
to a free ticke

The report found that the Company's entry into a market often caused the revenue of other airlines serving the market to fall by half, even as traffic volume increased. It further asserted that the industry's revenue would have been as much as $3 billion higher in 1992 if Southwest hadn't been making air travel more affordable.

To illustrate the point, the DOT looked at eight city pairs in California, including three that the Company served. It found that Southwest's low fares and high-frequency service enabled the carrier to dominate air traffic in the state in just three and a half years. In fact, Southwest controlled 80 percent of all the traffic between the Los Angeles and San Francisco areas even though San Francisco was a competitor's hub and Southwest didn't fly there at the time (it served the area through Oakland).

In the markets served by Southwest, traffic increased and fares went down. In the markets it didn't serve, the results were the opposite.

It wasn't just California. The government found the same thing happened in other markets across the country. Dubbed "the Southwest Effect," these findings validated the effectiveness of the Company's quest to make air travel more affordable and give more people the freedom to fly.

Of course, a lot has changed since then. Other airlines have gone through bankruptcy, using the process to cut costs so they could try to compete with Southwest. New entrants have come along trying to beat the Company at the low-fare game. But the Southwest Effect remains true.

Researchers at the Massachusetts Institute of Technology revisited the study in 2013 and found that Southwest was still driving fares lower and increasing traffic.

In 2014, Southwest was finally out from under most Wright Amendment restrictions, and it added dozens of new nonstop flights from Dallas (Love Field). Suddenly, finally, its competitors at the Dallas/Fort Worth International Airport (DFW) felt compelled to do the same. Guess what? Two years later, annual traffic at both airports serving the Dallas-Fort Worth area—Love Field and DFW—had soared 37 percent, rising by more than 5 million local customers. And those fliers saved a combined $920 million a year because of the lower fares. Those were the findings of yet another follow-up report, "The Southwest Effect Revisited," released in 2017 by researchers at the University of Virginia and Campbell-Hill Aviation Group.

That study also found that average one-way fares to Washington, D.C. (Reagan National) had dropped $122 and to New York (LaGuardia) $118 since Southwest started serving those airports. On average, passengers had spent $53 less per fare for flights to 34 different markets.

Although the Dallas example stood out, the report examined a total of 109 nonstop markets that Southwest entered between 2012 and 2015. The median fares declined by 15 percent, and passenger traffic rose by 28 percent.

In other words, after all these years, the Southwest Effect is still as effective as ever.

↑
Service map released June 2021. For up-to-date system information, including scheduled nonstop and connecting service for any given Southwest city, please visit Southwest.com® >Flight >Route Map.

Attack of the Copycats

When competitors tried to copy its low-fare service, Southwest was ready for battle.

British writer Charles Caleb Colton wrote that "imitation is the sincerest form of flattery." He obviously never worked in the airline business.

By 1994, the success of Southwest's low-cost philosophy had caught rivals' attention, and some tried to copy what Southwest did with the goal of beating it at its own game.

While the Company was making money and winning new Customers, many of its bigger rivals were racking up losses. "So, they woke up and knew they had to do something about this new competition," said Gary Kelly, who was then Vice President Finance and Chief Financial Officer. "Think about that—this is the entire industry that's almost conspiring together to attack Southwest."

One aggressive attack came from Shuttle by United, a low-cost airline-within-an-airline that directly competed with Southwest in California, offering fares as low as $19 one-way. Initially, the parent carrier assigned 25 aircraft to the operation—all Boeing 737s—and said Shuttle flights would offer no meals, one class of seating, low fares, and high-frequency flights between major cities in the Golden State. Sound familiar?

Southwest was ready. Its acquisition of Morris Air in 1993 had given it additional aircraft to use in markets it suspected would be targeted.

Herb addressed Employees as if he were leading troops into battle. Indeed, some Employees in California and at the Albuquerque Reservations Center even showed up for work in combat fatigues and battle helmets. Herb wrote a letter titled "Commencement of Hostilities," outlining what the Company was up against:

> *United has, on hand, over $1,000,000,000 in cash; can cross-subsidize its efforts against Southwest with revenues derived from its worldwide service; and has substantially reduced its costs by recently obtaining substantial wage and benefit reductions from most of its employees.*
>
> *In addition to our stock price, our wages, our benefits, our job security, our expansion opportunities, and, foremost, our pride of accomplishment as our nation's best airline are all on the line as the war begins. ...*

And while this major competitor might have started with 25 planes, its 737 fleet comprised 125 planes, meaning it had 100 more aircraft "to be hurled against us, at a later date," Herb wrote. At one point, the competition threatened to create 100 departures a day from Chicago (Midway), where Southwest had battled to gain a stronghold in the 1980s.

The airline-within-an-airline concept wasn't unique and had been developed by Southwest's old nemesis Texas Air (a merger of Texas International with Continental Airlines), which had attempted to create an hourly shuttle between Los Angeles and San Jose in 1985. It scrapped the idea a year later. By 1993, Continental decided to try again, developing "Continental Lite." But the service operated primarily out of Cleveland and Greensboro, North Carolina, making it less of a frontal assault. Other carriers also tested the idea with concepts such as Delta Express and USAir's MetroJet. (United even tried a second time, in 2008, when it introduced "Ted," an airline-within-an-airline that targeted leisure destinations. It ended the experiment a year later.)

This was more than a fare war. Combined with rivals' efforts to kick Southwest off their computerized reservation systems, it was an escalation of the war the Company had been waging since it first started: its fight for the right to exist. Southwest's competitors tried to crush it in the 1970s and largely ignored it in the 1980s, but by the 1990s, frightened by its success, they again seemed determined to try to knock it out of the skies.

"There seems to be an opinion out there that Southwest is somehow immune to competition from the majors—that they leave us alone," Herb said. "I say to people: 'Hey, they don't just launch low prices against us; they launch whole business divisions.' What do you think these airlines-within-airlines are all about?"

None of the tactics worked. The airline-within-an-airline trend was fading by 1995. "We had very solid earnings and sort of escaped this conspiracy, if you will," Gary said.

"They didn't stop there, but at least in terms of addressing the head-to-head competition, they could not compete with us. They didn't have the cost structure, they didn't have the service, so that was abandoned."

While the airlines-within-airlines managed to cut costs, they also alienated customers. Southwest's rivals had become so focused on cost, they forgot about things like customer service. But the biggest reason they failed was because they didn't have Southwest's Employees or its Culture, which prioritized taking care of People and which reflected, by that time, more than a quarter century of fighting for survival. During the battle for California, Employees implemented a program called "Helping Hands," in which Southwest People volunteered to go to California to help lighten the load on Employees there who were often pulling double shifts. The Company's competitors might imitate its cost structure or fares, but they couldn't replicate its shared commitment, dedication, and *esprit de corps*.

After 15 months, United threw in the towel on the Shuttle experiment. Rather than eroding Southwest's Customer base in California, it had strengthened it. The Company was about to report its most profitable year ever, and, as of 2020, has been the largest carrier in California for the last 20 years.

By January 1996, Herb had moved on, focused on expanding into Florida, a market he'd coveted for more than a decade. Florida's market looked then a lot like California's in 1989: Fares were high, intrastate service was poor, and the state's geography was a natural for high-frequency, low-fare service. As Herb was concentrating on how to approach the expansion, another Executive interrupted him.

"Guess what happens if you pick up your phone and call 1-800-SOUTHWEST?"

"You mean 1-800-I FLY SWA," Herb replied. "That's our reservations number."

"I know," the other Executive said, "but guess what happens if you call 1-800-SOUTHWEST?"

Herb dialed the number. After four rings, someone answered.

"Shuttle by United reservations. This is Todd."

After a moment of stunned silence, Herb exploded with his trademark laugh. The world's biggest airline had been reduced to impersonating Southwest—the very Company it had hoped to beat. As the laughter subsided, Herb turned back to his desk.

"Let's talk about Florida," he said.

The (Second) Battle of Baltimore

By 1993, Southwest was looking for new growth markets, and the biggest untapped opportunity lay to the east. It added service to Baltimore/Washington (BWI), making it a coast-to-coast carrier for the first time.

Once again, the Southwest Effect kicked in. Fares at BWI fell 70 percent, and the number of passengers increased sevenfold. Before Southwest started flying there, the average fare from Baltimore to Chicago's O'Hare airport was $156.35, and the number of passengers flown annually was more than 7,600. Chicago's Midway airport accounted for just 552 passengers. After it had been flying from Baltimore to Midway for a year, the number of passengers soared to almost 10,800, and the average one-way fare fell to less than $47. Interestingly, while the O'Hare traffic also increased—to more than 13,000 passengers—the average one-way fare fell there, too, dropping to almost $63 as Southwest's competitors tried to match its pricing.

Like the city's famous crab cakes, Southwest's move into Baltimore was wildly popular—and it opened up new markets and made the airline a coast-to-coast carrier.

↑
On July 14, 1993, Herb—shown here with then-Maryland Gov. William Schaefer, who was clearly ready for anything—announced Southwest would set sail for Baltimore/Washington later that year. The city became the base from which Southwest expanded up and down the East Coast.

The foray into Baltimore/Washington brought Southwest squarely onto the home turf of USAir. Southwest had battled USAir in California, and the other carrier eventually surrendered that market; but at BWI, USAir decided to take a stand. Not only did it match Southwest's fares from day one, but by 1998, USAir had developed a low-cost airline-within-an-airline called MetroJet.

Once again, Herb, who was Chairman, President, and CEO at the time, invoked military language in addressing Employees. He compared Southwest's showdown with MetroJet to the battle for Fort McHenry at the end of the War of 1812, the skirmish that inspired Francis Scott Key to write *The Star-Spangled Banner*. Herb recounted that famous battle and declared that this would be the Company's Fort McHenry—the second battle for Baltimore.

"At the conclusion of this 'Battle,' our flag, the flag of Southwest Airlines, MUST still fly over the ramparts of Baltimore!" he wrote.

MetroJet planned to hit Southwest with 54 737-200s, matching it plane for plane on most routes and charging fares that were equal or in some cases even lower than Southwest's. Just as with the Shuttle by United battle in California, Herb rallied the troops, noting everything the Company had on the line—jobs, profitability, expansion plans.

"There is a LOT at stake in the Battle of Baltimore," he wrote. "The outcome of this latest attack on Southwest by another of the Big Seven carriers is just as important to ALL of us as the result of our West Coast war with Shuttle by United."

Of course, the outcome was much the same. Southwest's flag did, indeed, continue to fly over Baltimore. While MetroJet hung around for a few years, USAir announced in September 2001, after the 9/11 terror attacks, it would shut it down.

Meanwhile, BWI became Southwest's base on the East Coast from which it expanded into markets such as Manchester, New Hampshire; Providence, Rhode Island; and cities in Florida, beginning with Tampa and Fort Lauderdale/Hollywood in January 1996. Many airline observers thought the Company would never enter the Eastern Corridor, where airports tend to be more congested and some have controlled landing slots. At the same time, they worried that the Southwest Effect would fade as it moved eastward.

Far from it. Our Employees sported T-shirts declaring "Welcome to BWI: The Beast of the East," and many still refer to themselves that way.

"We have been very forceful and resilient, but there is really no new trick in going into Manchester or Providence and making them immediate successes in the traditional Southwest way," Herb said. "Why would people think that going into the East Coast market and reducing fares by 70 percent is new for us?"

In fact, as Southwest grew in the East, it eventually moved into the types of airports it once avoided—congested, slot controlled—such as New York (LaGuardia), added in 2009, and Washington, D.C. (Reagan National), added in 2012. "Our network had matured to a point that our Customers began requesting service to these popular locations," said retired Vice President Airport Affairs Bob Montgomery. "Our expansion worked tremendously. Washington National has been such a huge success, and LaGuardia is a huge success."

southwest

Rocky Mountain Fly

After initiating service in Denver, Southwest increased traffic more than any other airline in the Mile High City and was ready to "shred" the competition.

Thar may be gold in them thar hills, but it took Southwest awhile to mine success in Denver. The Company first began flying to the Mile High City's old Stapleton International Airport in 1983, but it pulled out of the market three years later because of frequent delays.

A decade later, when Southwest acquired Morris Air in 1993, it still hadn't warmed up to Denver, withdrawing Morris' operations there just as the city prepared to open Denver International Airport. Southwest balked at the hefty $16 per passenger fee the city planned to charge airlines to pay for the new state-of-the-art facility.

Things changed in 2005. United Airlines, which operated a hub in Denver, filed for bankruptcy and cut its fares. At the same time, the airport lowered its fees to a more manageable $12 per passenger. Southwest had planes available because of reduced service to New Orleans after Hurricane Katrina, which hit in August of that year, and in January 2006, the Company redeployed some of those aircraft to begin service to Denver.

Its operations there grew rapidly, in part because of the pullback by United and the other local carrier, Frontier Airlines, which spent much of 2008 and 2009 in bankruptcy. Southwest tried to buy Frontier in 2009, but the deal fell through. By the end of 2009, Southwest had surpassed both Frontier and United in Denver in originating and final destination passengers, and by 2011, it was No. 1.

"United was bankrupt; they went into decline there, and we just ran right past them," Chairman and CEO Gary Kelly said. "Our success in Denver really ramped up as time went by."

Southwest reached 200 departing flights a day faster than it did in any other city.

Between 2000 and 2018, no other airline increased passenger traffic more at any one airport than Southwest did in Denver.

"Denver is the fastest-growing city [in terms of Passenger traffic] in our history," Bob Jordan, Executive Vice President and Incoming CEO (2022), said in 2013 when he was Chief Commercial Officer. By then, Denver had overtaken Houston (Hobby) and Dallas (Love Field) in the number of daily Southwest flights.

The Company opened Pilot and Flight Attendant Crew bases in Denver in 2012, and before the 2020 COVID-19 pandemic, Southwest had more than 4,000 Employees there. In 2019, it announced plans for a $100 million maintenance hangar that, with more than 130,000 square feet, could accommodate three 737s simultaneously.

By then, Southwest had 32 percent of the Denver market, which helped make the city one of the fastest-growing aviation markets in the country. From 2015 to 2020, the number of passengers arriving in and departing from Denver increased by more than 15,000 per day.

The pandemic and the worldwide grounding of the 737 MAX 8 stalled Southwest's plans to add 100 more flights a day in Denver in 2020, but the city remains key for the Company. As the market recovers, Southwest hopes to take its Denver operations to new heights.

←
A Ramp Agent guides an aircraft pushing back from a gate in Denver in 2018.

→
The sun shines brightly on a Southwest flight in Denver.

One LUV

A rubber duck became a symbol for celebrating one of the greatest unions in airline history—Southwest and AirTran.

Over the years, Southwest had grown accustomed to being the scrappy underdog of the airline business. But by 2004, it had become the nation's largest domestic air carrier in terms of domestic originating passengers boarded. To keep growing and adjusting to changes—such as the post-9/11 security regulations that affected many of its short-haul routes—it had to shift its thinking. The Company needed to expand its longer-haul routes and increase efforts to attract business travelers. To do that, it needed to go where demand led, even if that meant slightly adjusting its strategy. While Southwest had never tried to be all things to all people, it also recognized that times—and its stature—had changed.

"If you want to grow and you want to win more Customers, you've got to go where they want to go," Chairman and CEO Gary Kelly said. That meant entering busier airports and more heavily traveled markets that the Company had avoided in the past.

SOUTHWEST
ONE
LUV

airTran
ONE
LUV

With that in mind, Southwest inaugurated service to key airports in 2009, including Minneapolis/St. Paul, New York (LaGuardia), Boston Logan, and Milwaukee.

A year later, it found an opportunity to accelerate growth through a tactic it had used only a few times before: an acquisition. In September 2010, Southwest announced plans to acquire AirTran Holdings Inc., the parent company of AirTran Airways (AirTran), in a deal valued at $3.4 billion. It was, by far, the biggest acquisition in Southwest's history. With little overlap between route systems, AirTran gave Southwest access to airports such as Atlanta and Washington, D.C. (Reagan National), increasing its capacity by about 25 percent. The transaction, which closed in May 2011, also strengthened the Company's position at the three destinations added a few years earlier.

"We were able to go in, restructure their routes and their business, boost their profitability, which boosted our overall profitability, hit our profit goals, [and] get us back on a growth trajectory," Gary said.

"It's just been a fabulous acquisition."

In addition, AirTran's experience flying internationally allowed Southwest to launch the next major phase of its growth, adding destinations such as Aruba in 2014 and Havana in 2016 (its 100th destination at the time), as well as others in Mexico and the Caribbean.

←
At a celebration in Atlanta on May 2, 2011, (from left) former AirTran CEO Bob Fornaro, Gary, and now-Executive Vice President and Incoming CEO (2022) Bob Jordan offer a toast to AirTran Crew Members and Southwest Employees. Bob Jordan was named AirTran President and oversaw the integration.

Airline mergers often can be difficult, especially for the employees. That's part of the reason Southwest took its time, carefully integrating the two airlines. The final AirTran flight, from Atlanta to Tampa, occurred at the end of 2014. In the three years from the time the deal closed until the AirTran name disappeared, the two groups of Employees had time to get to know each other.

To celebrate the effort of bringing the two families together, Southwest used the slogan "One LUV," and a little rubber duck became its mascot. (Southwest already had its own line of branded rubber ducks that were used in a New Hire rubber duck derby. AirTran's white-and-teal color scheme was added to one side of a new duck model with the familiar Southwest canyon blue and red on the other side.) Southwest also launched the One LUV tour, which visited 15 AirTran locations to educate Employees (who were all referred to as "Crew Members" at AirTran) on Living and Working the Southwest Way. For one meeting in Baltimore, an AirTran Flight Attendant took a three-hour train ride to attend; a Reservations Agent brought cake; and a Gate Agent drove more than an hour to learn more about the Company he was joining. It meant that much.

A "WingMate Program" randomly paired Southwest Employees and almost 8,000 AirTran Employees, much like pen pals, and helped them to understand the Cultures of both Companies and to forge a new one together. Today, they are all Southwest Employees, but no one's forgotten the unique Culture AirTran brought to Southwest and how it made everyone stronger.

Hawaii at Last

Southwest featured traditional Hawaiian celebrations when it inaugurated service to the Islands in 2019.

Since he became CEO in 2004, the one question Gary Kelly had been asked most often was when Southwest would arrive in Hawaii.

When the Company polled its Customers, they consistently listed Hawaii as one of their most-desired destinations. Employees dreamed of using their travel privileges to vacation there or even moving to the Islands while keeping their jobs with Southwest.

While the Company never stopped thinking about the Islands, it would be more than a decade before the possibility of flying there would force any decisions. The announcement finally came at a Spirit Party at a Southern California theme park in 2017, when Gary, sporting an Aloha shirt, took the stage in front of 10,000 Employees and guests, joined by Cheryl Hughey, then Managing Director Culture, and Chief Operating Officer Mike Van de Ven. The excited crowd welcomed the news with chants of "A-lo-ha! A-lo-ha!" Later, Southwest President Tom Nealon joined the conversation via a livestream from Waikiki Beach in Honolulu, accompanied by Hawaii Governor David Ige.

Southwest still had to address the regulatory and federal flight safety requirements, but by planning service well in advance, the Company had time to build its fleet and its capabilities. The Federal Aviation Administration's (FAA) "Extended Operations," or ETOPS, authorization would be needed.

ETOPS basically means two-engine aircraft must be certified to fly over places that are more than 60 minutes from an adequate airport (which are nonexistent in the Pacific Ocean) with one engine inoperative.

↓
Captains Michael Styer and Rob Evers on the flight deck of the inaugural flight to Hawaii.

To meet these requirements, a Team of subject matter experts, led by Senior Director Regulatory Operations Steve Christl, hammered out a process to adapt the Company's existing systems and incorporate the new ETOPS procedures and technology into its network.

Once the intended service became public, Employee training began, and the Company conducted tabletop exercises with the FAA, clearing the way for validation flights. Then, a Washington budget battle in late 2018 triggered a government shutdown, which stalled the certification process.

Soon after the government reopened in January 2019, Southwest began a series of validation flights. With FAA officials onboard, it put its planes through a series of simulated crises to test Crew response. The simulations included "depressurization" events, forced "emergency landings" at different airports, and even a bird strike. Southwest Employees' actions were carefully monitored and recorded during these simulations, which continued over 10 separate FAA test flights.

The Company passed with flying colors. But even before the tests were completed, the Southwest Effect had kicked in. Established carriers in Hawaii cut fares to entice passengers who had been waiting until Southwest's flights went on sale to book their vacations. Residents of Hawaii were thrilled, too, because the Company's interisland fares would bring much-needed competition to that market. By the time Southwest started flying, fares had fallen an average of 17 percent. Seats sold out within minutes of the Company's news release announcing fares and service.

The inaugural flight left Oakland bound for Honolulu (Oahu) on March 17, 2019, with Captains Michael Styer and Rob Evers on the flight deck. A venerated *kahu* (honored guardian) and cultural historian performed a ceremonial blessing of the flight and the plane itself.

For two years before the launch of service, Southwest sent Teams to Hawaii to learn the culture. They met with *kupuna* (elders) on each island and other influential members of the community to ensure the Company launched service in a culturally relevant and respectful way. Cultural practitioners from Hawaii came to Southwest's Headquarters in Dallas to provide training in Hawaiian culture.

During all those years when Gary was asked if Southwest would fly to Hawaii, he knew it wasn't a question of *if*, but *when* and *how*.

It took awhile, and a lot of dedication and persistence by Southwest's People, but they finally got him his answer.

↓
Honolulu (Oahu) Station Employees celebrate the start of revenue service in March 2019.

Southwest Heart in Action

Living by The Golden Rule

Southwest

Adopt-A-Pilot
City Life
Take Flight
Live Life
Pure Beauty
adopt A Pilot
Set Your Heart on This
Love
CELEBRATING 15 YEARS
SOUTHWEST AIRLINES!
adopt A Pilot
SOUTHWEST AIRLINES
adopt A Pilot

Flying Lessons

Through Southwest's Adopt-A-Pilot® program, Pilots share their love of flying and inspire the next generation of airline employees.

David Childs developed a love for aviation at a young age. After he became a Pilot for Southwest in 2000, he wanted to find a way to ignite the same passion for flying in young people that his father had instilled in him. He saw an internal advertisement for Southwest's Adopt-A-Pilot® program, which began in 1997. The four-week course teaches thousands of students, primarily in cities that Southwest serves, what it's like to fly planes. Pilots lead lessons in life values, career planning, geography, scientific processes, and aerodynamics.

The program was exactly what David was looking for, and he spent five years teaching at Bridge Creek Elementary near Oklahoma City. He developed activities in which students raced paper airplanes to learn about aerodynamics. He shared stories about the places he flew, and he taped off the floor to make runways and taxiways for imaginary aircraft.

3 HRS
09:00
12:00
N
W E
S

One of his students was Jessica Mitchell. Before David started working with the class, Jessica dreaded math, science, and geography. But after learning how these skills could be applied to the real world—and a real job—she had a change of heart. The airplane races and other lessons captured her interest, and the summer after her fifth-grade year, Jessica flew on an airplane for the first time. (It was a Southwest flight, of course.)

She was hooked, and in 2018, Jessica began her career as a Southwest Flight Attendant based in Denver. Her passion for flying, which David first sparked at Bridge Creek Elementary, had become a life-changing experience for Jessica.

The Adopt-A-Pilot program has remained popular with Southwest Pilots and the schools that adopt them. Every year, the Company's Pilots turn their daily duties into a learning experience in classrooms across the country. They also remind students of the importance of school and how hard work and commitment are essential to achieving dreams. Pilots also share their experiences that show students how science, geography, and math are applied in real life.

While it's not possible to know how many students have gone on to careers in aviation, the story of David and Jessica isn't unique.

Tim Shawcross always loved flying when he was a kid, but it was only after his father visited his fifth-grade class that he thought about becoming a pilot. Tim's father, Al, a Southwest Captain, had been active in Adopt-A-Pilot for about a year before he went to Tim's school to talk to students about the science of flying.

Seeing the excitement in the students' eyes, Al continued teaching that same fifth-grade class long after Tim moved on to other grades. Tim, for his part, never lost the sense of inspiration he felt hearing his father talk about life on the flight deck. Years later, he started his own career in aviation and became a First Officer for a regional airline based in Utah. Now, Tim and Al teach the class together.

Like Al, Atif Fareed served as a Pilot mentor for his son Adam's third- and fifth-grade classes. The excitement the Southwest Pilot saw in the children inspired him to keep teaching, and Adam credits his father's lessons with inspiring his own interest in flying.

Years later, Adam became a pilot for a regional airline, and father and son teamed up to teach an Adopt-A-Pilot class at Leaders Preparatory School.

"The feeling of giving back to students is rewarding, and I hope my story can inspire students to reach new heights," Adam said.

That, of course, is what the Adopt-A-Pilot program is all about.

←
A Southwest First Officer leads a discussion in an elementary school classroom in 2015.

Courage Amid Crisis

On 9/11, Southwest Employees supported Customers and one another to pull the Company through one of the country's darkest moments.

Just after 8 a.m. on September 11, 2001, then-Director Flight and Dispatch Greg Wells was on his way to Headquarters, driving down Interstate 35 and listening to sports talk radio. Suddenly, the broadcast was interrupted: A large plane had crashed into the World Trade Center in New York City, and the building was burning.

At Headquarters, Gary Kelly, who was then Executive Vice President and Chief Financial Officer, walked into a conference room near his office and saw the video of smoke billowing from one of the Twin Towers. As he watched, a second plane slammed into the adjacent building.

"Everyone knew something was wrong, something was bad," Gary recalled. He walked to Colleen's office—she was President then—and they quickly assembled a Team in their crisis center, which was also the boardroom. CEO Jim Parker, who had just moved into that role less than three months earlier, was there, as was Herb, who was Chairman.

When Greg arrived at Headquarters, he headed straight for the Dispatch Department, expecting pandemonium. Instead, the room was shrouded in eerie silence.

"All you could hear was radio communication because all of our Dispatchers were heads down, communicating with flights they were responsible for dispatching, landing them in the nearest suitable airport," he said. "[It was] probably the most stressful thing I ever went through, the most confusing thing I ever went through."

As the day unfolded, the scope of the tragedy came into focus. America had been attacked by terrorists who hijacked four commercial jetliners and flew two of them into the Twin Towers of the World Trade Center in New York City. A third crashed into the Pentagon, and a fourth went down in a field in Pennsylvania after passengers onboard fought back against their hijackers. Everyone onboard the planes was killed, and thousands more in the buildings and the surrounding areas died or were injured. The Federal Aviation Administration immediately grounded more than 4,500 commercial aircraft in U.S. air space.

"That was tense ... because no one knew what was going to happen next," Gary said. "It was this odd feeling. There was nothing moving at Southwest."

For airline employees, the attacks added insult to the anger, outrage, and sorrow the country was feeling. Not only had they been attacked on their own soil, but the terrorists had turned their own equipment—commercial jets—into a weapon.

With the immediate grounding of all flights, Executive Vice President and Chief of Operations Jim Wimberly scrambled to account for all Southwest planes, now scattered across the country. One plane could not be found. "We're thinking, 'Are we in a Pennsylvania field? Where is our airplane?'" Greg said. "We finally found out it had diverted offline." The plane had landed in Grand Rapids, Michigan, a city Southwest didn't serve yet.

Back in the boardroom—which doubled as the command center—the severity of the situation was sinking in. On top of what this meant to our Leaders and our Employees personally, it presented an imminent financial crisis for the Company that had to be addressed immediately. When nothing moves at an airline, there's no money coming in, and Gary quickly had to determine how much cash was on hand, what bills could be deferred, and what other commitments Southwest had. At the time, no one knew how long planes would be grounded, or if anyone would be willing to get on one once flights resumed.

Within days, the Company delayed deliveries of 11 new 737s and halted a planned project to expand its headquarters facilities. But one decision was made almost immediately: Southwest would cut every cost it could, save every possible dime, before it would cut pay or lay off People.

"We decided that day that the last thing that we would do would be to consider layoffs—the last thing, not the first thing," Gary said. Jim Parker sent an email to all 32,000 Employees at the time, assuring them they had a job and the Company would keep paying their salaries for as long as it could.

"The confidence instilled by that kind of communication from the CEO in a time of crisis, when People's heads are spinning, [was] one of the great masterstrokes of Leadership and of the Core Values of Southwest," said Dave Ridley, retired Senior Vice President Business Development.

Colleen worked the phones for hours, helping to locate the planes, Crews, and Customers scattered by the crisis. Pilots and Flight Attendants found hotels for Customers. Colleen called one hotel, looking for the Pilot of a particular flight. "This is Colleen Barrett, and I'm from Southwest Airlines and I understand that you have our Employees and a load full of Customers at your hotel," she said. The desk clerk said he did. Colleen asked if she could be connected to the Pilot's room. The clerk said the Pilot wasn't there.

"He rented a bus, and he said that there was too much doom and gloom on TV," the clerk said. "He didn't want his Passengers to see it, so he's taking them to a movie."

"You are kidding me," Colleen said.

"No," the clerk replied. "And he bought them pizza, and they're eating pizza on the bus."

In the following days, Southwest Employees grieved along with the entire nation. While 9/11 disrupted other airlines—leading to layoffs, pay and benefit cuts, and even bankruptcy—many of the Company's Senior Leaders suspended their own salaries but kept paying Employees. Even so, some Employees chose to give up their pay. As part of the Pledge to LUV program, Employees donated up to 32 hours of pay each and Flight Crews up to 28 trips each to help the Company get back on its feet.

Meanwhile, some of Southwest's most loyal Customers and family members of Employees who had free flight privileges sent checks to help the Company get through the hard times.

The Company resumed television advertising eight days after the attacks—ahead of most competitors—and the message was simple: When you're ready to fly again, we're here for you. Colleen did the voice-over, without a script, speaking from the heart and expressing the sentiment she was feeling.

The attacks derailed what had been shaping up to be a banner year. In the first eight months, the Company became the largest domestic carrier, with 63 million originating Passengers. After the attacks, its People pulled together to get it through the crisis and get operations back to normal as quickly as possible. It wasn't easy. The Company cut every expense it could, and even then, the fear of bankruptcy lingered. But gradually, things improved.

On September 14, Southwest's planes returned to the skies. The Company went ahead with plans to begin service to Norfolk, Virginia, the next month. Not only did it keep all its People, it hired everyone who was in training or onboarding for a job at the time. It even went on to make a profit in the fourth quarter.

Gradually the Company began to see signs that things were getting back to normal. But there was another, brighter sign of hope: the way its People responded.

"We didn't panic," Gary said. "In a pinch, in a crisis, we all treated each other with respect. We all worked together."

TUSKEGEE AIRMEN, INC.

Standing Up for Diversity

From celebrating the Tuskegee Airmen (who gave Herb an honorary membership and jacket) to providing flights home for Hispanic students, Southwest supports diverse communities.

As the Southwest 737 taxied toward the gate in Montgomery, Alabama, on October 29, 2005, airport fire trucks shot arcs of water over the plane as it passed, a traditional aviation salute for an honored passenger.

The casket of civil rights leader Rosa Parks, who five days earlier had passed away at age 92, had been placed in the cargo hold.

On the flight deck, Captain Lou Freeman, who had joined Southwest in 1980, was moved by the gesture, pointing out that while fire hoses were saluting Mrs. Parks that day, 50 years earlier similar water hoses were used very differently against those who advocated for rights in Montgomery and elsewhere.

"It makes you want to tear up and cry when you think of what she did and what she accomplished," said Lou, Southwest's Chief Pilot in Chicago (Midway) at the time and the first African American Chief Pilot in the industry. "She told us all to stand up for our rights."

The NAACP had developed the idea for Mrs. Parks' final flight, and the organization immediately thought of Southwest as the transportation partner. The Company had worked with local NAACP chapters for years as part of its community outreach efforts and had also supported the National Great Blacks in Wax Museum in promoting a display of wax figures of historic African Americans for the NAACP's national convention.

Southwest for years has backed diverse communities through a variety of programs. Specifically, the Company has long supported efforts to commemorate the history of the Tuskegee Airmen, a group of about 1,000 African American pilots and other aviation personnel who trained at Tuskegee Army Air Field in Mrs. Parks' hometown of Tuskegee, Alabama, between 1941 and 1946, and flew combat missions in World War II. Just seven months before Mrs. Parks' death, Southwest had hosted 14 of the surviving Airmen with a heroes' celebration at the Company's Dallas maintenance facility.

Since 2005, Southwest has partnered with the Hispanic Association of Colleges and Universities (HACU) to sponsor the ¡Lánzate!/Take Off! Higher Education Travel Award Program to provide funds for Hispanic college students who can't afford to fly home between semesters. The program invites college and graduate students who live more than 200 miles from their homes to submit an essay about the hidden connections among family, travel, and educational excellence. Winners of the contest receive one to four Southwest round trip tickets to help them reconnect with family during times of need or celebration. Since the partnership started, Southwest has donated more than 4,000 tickets to recipients across the country.

In 2018, after Southwest began flying to destinations in Latin America and the Caribbean, Southwest became the official airline of the National Diversity Council.

Because of its deep and long-standing commitment to diversity, equity, and inclusion, when Colleen, who was President at the time, heard the NAACP was asking for Southwest's help in honoring Mrs. Parks, she immediately approved for Southwest to donate a plane and fuel and provide a Crew (who volunteered their time free of charge) to help make the final trip for Mrs. Parks possible. Karen Price-Ward, Community Outreach National Strategic Relationships Lead at the time, took over the planning duties, working with Southwest's Charters Department and enlisting Lou.

Karen and Lou assembled a diverse Crew of volunteers for the three-day trip, including Flight Deck Crew Captain Richard, First Officer Trevor, and Inflight Supervisors Yolanda, Rita, and Renee.

Lou said he and the rest of the Crew were honored to volunteer for the flight.

"It's been historic—a wondrous reflective part of history," he said. "You realize you're touching something that's going to last forever."

Lou retired in 2017, but that flight 12 years earlier still stands out as one of the most memorable moments in his illustrious 36-year career—and in Southwest's first 50 years.

*(*Southwest Airlines would like to thank the Rosa and Raymond Parks Institute for Self Development, whom Southwest partnered with in 2005. It was truly an honor for Southwest to serve Mrs. Parks, her family, and the Black community in this way, and we thank the Institute for the rights to commemorate this moment in Southwest and U.S. history.)*

↑
In Montgomery, Alabama, a water cannon salute welcomes the flight carrying the remains of Rosa Parks in November 2005.

Southwest®

Pet Project

Southwest paws-itively loves animals. The airline has flown multiple rescue flights to help dogs and cats stranded by natural disasters.

In 2017, Captain David "Fig" Newton got a call from his Chief Pilot. Southwest was planning to fly a planeload of supplies to Puerto Rico to help with relief efforts in the wake of Hurricane Maria. A lot of dogs had been displaced by the storm, shelters were overwhelmed, and Southwest was considering flying a group of rescue dogs back on the return trip.

"I'm in," said David, who had joined Southwest in 1988.

"Well," his Chief Pilot said, "I haven't told you anything about it."

"It doesn't matter," David replied. "I'm doing it."

David and his wife, Diane, had been involved in dog rescue efforts for years, and they'd even outfitted their private plane specifically to transport dog kennels. They flew dogs from areas where shelters were full to other regions of the country where people were looking for pets to adopt.

For the Puerto Rico flight, Southwest worked with Lucky Dog Animal Rescue in Arlington, Virginia. The group had approached Chairman and CEO Gary Kelly, who said the Company would like to help. Southwest then teamed up with the Sato Project, a rescue group in Puerto Rico that helped identify the animals to transport.

"There were a lot of dogs who were left homeless and ended up in shelters," David said. "They wanted to make room for more dogs coming in, so they needed these dogs to get to the United States, where they could be re-homed, so they ... wouldn't have to euthanize any."

David, the Flight Attendants, and other Employees who helped monitor the dogs on the return trip volunteered for the flight. The plane left Baltimore/Washington (BWI) with 10,000 pounds of humanitarian supplies and returned with 62 dogs and cats, each in its own kennel strapped into a seat in the cabin.

↑
Captains Barnes Pruett and David "Fig" Newton get puppy cuddles after a dedicated pet rescue flight in early 2018 from San Juan to Baltimore/Washington (BWI) after the devastation of Hurricane Maria.

"That was a big Companywide effort to make sure everything was done correctly and in compliance," David said.

"It took a lot of effort by the Executive Office, in coordination with the Puerto Rico Station, the Baltimore Station, Network Operations Control (NOC), and Flight Ops to coordinate and put this together. I just happened to be lucky enough to be up at the front of the airplane."

Organizers had to coordinate who was going to unload the aircraft and where it should park when it landed in Puerto Rico. Rather than pulling up to a gate, the jet was unloaded, and the pets brought aboard at a fixed-base operator facility at the airport.

Although he had never flown a Southwest pet rescue flight before, David had helped coordinate one in which a soon-to-be-retired 737-300 flew dogs and cats, left homeless in New Orleans by Hurricane Katrina in 2005, from Austin to San Diego.

Southwest made several flights to assist in the relief efforts after Katrina, rescuing displaced animals and providing support to its own Employees in the aftermath of that catastrophic storm. In 2012, Southwest partnered with SeaWorld to fly 60 cats and dogs from Newark to the Helen Woodward Animal Center in San Diego after a sudden increase in displaced pets in shelters from the greater New York area because of Superstorm Sandy.

Southwest also has a long history of flying animals beyond disaster rescues. Over the years, it transported penguins and other marine animals under its partnership with SeaWorld, and in 2009, it initiated a new program, "Pets Are Welcome on Southwest," or PAWS. The program allows Customers to bring small dogs and cats onboard, for an additional fee, provided they remain properly stowed in an approved carrier. Later the same year, Southwest started selling branded pet carriers, which have been popular with Customers.

Of course, the Company also accommodates trained service animals, such as seeing-eye dogs as well as dogs that help their owners maintain their balance or alert them to impending seizures. Southwest doesn't allow pets to fly in the cargo holds, because its 737s don't have heated or pressurized cargo areas, David said.

As for the rescue efforts, the legions of animal lovers who work for Southwest will continue to help when they can.

"I feel very fortunate that Southwest went out of its way to recognize that need and help these animals," David said.

↑
An all-volunteer Crew unloads puppies and kittens after a rescue flight from Houston (Hobby) to San Diego in the wake of Hurricane Harvey in 2017.

61
MAX. TOW SPEED
15 M.P.H.

A Special Flight

In 2019, a war hero was laid to rest after a homecoming that the Pilot, Captain Bryan Knight, had been waiting for most of his life.

On the morning of August 8, 2019, the normally bustling Dallas Love Field came to a standstill as Captain Bryan Knight rolled his Southwest 737 to a stop. Through the flight deck window, he could see people in the terminal looking out at the plane. Some were wiping away tears.

Inside the terminal, people pressed to the windows to see the arrival. Water cannons saluted the plane, and the Team on the ground stood at attention. A voice from air traffic control crackled over the radio: "From one Vietnam vet to another, welcome home."

Bryan, a Southwest Captain who retired in 2020, remembered the first time he had been to Dallas Love Field, in December 1966. It was the last time he would see his father, Roy Knight Jr.

9009
TOW

Bryan was 5 years old at the time, and he'd come with his mother to see Roy off. The elder Knight was headed to Southeast Asia to fly A-1 Skyraider missions into Vietnam.

About five months after Bryan and his father said goodbye, the family got word that Roy's plane had been shot down in enemy territory along the Ho Chi Minh Trail. In 1974, the U.S. government declared him killed in action.

Bryan joined the Reserve Officers' Training Corps at Texas Christian University and eventually trained as a pilot, flying the A-10 Thunderbolt, an updated version of the A-1 his father had flown. Bryan joined Southwest in 2000 and spent 20 years with the Company.

In 2019, a team from the Defense POW/MIA Accounting Agency was using a metal detector near a site in Laos that had previously been searched. They found physical remains, a dog tag chain, and parts of a helmet that included the lettering "MAJ KNI." Forensic testing confirmed that Roy had been found.

Bryan's family learned of the discovery in June, and preparations began to bring Roy's remains home. "When I first got the call, it was almost surreal," Bryan said.

"I really didn't think it would ever happen. Wow, you know, he's really coming home. We're going to be able to bring him back, and we're going to have a place where we can honor him."

Bryan wrote to his Chief Pilot and received permission to fly his father's remains home to Texas. When Roy's remains arrived in Oakland, California, Bryan was there to fly the last leg of the journey with his dad, 52 years after they'd last seen each other.

As Roy's flag-draped casket came off the plane, family members placed their hands on it and paid their respects. Roy's remains were taken to Cool, Texas, west of Fort Worth, where he was finally laid to rest.

The remains of Col. Roy A. Knight Jr., who was killed in the Vietnam War, are returned to Dallas aboard a special flight flown by his son, Southwest Captain Bryan Knight, in August 2019.

THANK YOU
SWA
Bark
window

Air Care

Southwest and its Partners provide transportation when patients and their families need to travel far from home for medical care.

In June 2016, a crowd gathered in the terminal at the Louis Armstrong New Orleans International Airport for a very special send-off. Levi Krystosek, who was 10 at the time, was flying to Philadelphia for a medical consultation. Levi has a rare form of dwarfism that prevents his bones from strengthening as he grows, leaving them unable to support his weight. Only 22 such cases had been confirmed in the world at the time, and Levi and his mother have had to travel around the country for medical monitoring and treatment. Through it all, Levi has inspired adults and caregivers nationwide and maintained a cheerful and Fun-LUVing attitude.

Levi arrived at the gate in a homemade pilot uniform and was greeted with red carpet and VIP treatment from Southwest, which also handed out treats for other Customers and provided a live band for Levi's send-off. As his plane left the gate, it was given a water cannon salute.

Southwest helped ease the financial burden of the frequent travel on Levi's mother through the Southwest Airlines Medical Transportation Grant Program, which the Company started in 2007. In Levi's case, Southwest partnered with a nonprofit that provides complimentary commercial air travel for seriously ill patients to visit specialists and receive treatment throughout the country. Through the end of 2020, Southwest had donated more than 96,500 round trip flights—an average of more than 6,400 flights a year—with a value of about $38.6 million.

"It's a wonderful program that provides more than free flights. It offers hope to patients and their families. And for some it has been life-changing, and for that I am truly humbled to be a part of it," said Senior Specialist Community Outreach Debbie Wafford.

No one knows exactly when the practice of helping Customers with medical needs got started, but it was encouraged by Herb and Colleen, and built on other programs, such as Southwest's long-standing support for Ronald McDonald Houses, which provide a home away from home for families of seriously ill children.

When families approached Southwest about flights for medical care, Colleen decided it was something the Company should do when possible.

"Prior to the program, we received calls directly from patients or their family members—a worried parent, a concerned husband or wife," Debbie said. "We listened to them and helped them because it was the right thing to do." As word got out, the number of calls increased, and Southwest helped as much as it could.

Changes in medical privacy laws, however, required a more formal approach.

"We realized that there was a great need out there, and we wanted to continue to help these folks, but we needed to do it differently," Debbie said.

Under the new system, hospitals and medical travel organizations apply for a grant of tickets from Southwest. These Partners then provide the tickets to patients based on need.

When the program started in 2007, the Company was working with three hospitals; in 2021, it's partnering with 75 nonprofit hospitals and several medical transport charities around the country.

But it's the patients who make the program worthwhile, Debbie said. Even though the program is coordinated through the hospitals, when patients arrive at the airport, they know that it's Southwest that's helping them. Debbie has a box of thank-you notes from the program's participants that she keeps on her desk.

"Without the assistance from the Southwest Airlines Medical Transportation Grant Program, I would be unable to receive the quality of care for my upcoming surgery," one cancer patient wrote. "This assistance has been a tremendous relief for me and my family."

"Thank you, thank you, thank you," wrote one self-employed grant recipient. "You have no idea how helpful this is. This [program] offers my son hope and a chance of living. I wasn't sure financially how I was going to do this. You have just lifted a heavy burden."

From Levi, to other children in need, to hundreds of other patients of all ages, the Medical Transportation Grant Program has made their struggles a little easier by connecting them with the care they need.

←
Levi Krystosek, in full pilot garb, talks to a reporter after Southwest rolled out the red carpet in his honor in 2016.

Hearts and Soles

James had no shoes. Like many children in rural Kenya, he walked barefoot everywhere he went, which left the soles of his feet prone to bites from sand fleas, known as jiggers. When the bites became infected, he couldn't walk to school.

In the summer of 2014, he received a new pair of slip-on shoes with a color scheme that might be familiar to Customers who flew Southwest as early as 2001—dark blue uppers and tan soles.

As the Company retrofitted its fleet, replacing its Spirit cabin seat covers with the new EVOLVE materials, it found itself with 43 acres of used seat leather. Rather than dumping all that in a landfill or shredding it, Southwest developed the LUV Seat program.

The Company realized that if it could get that leather to Kenya, it might be able to change the lives of children like James.

Making soccer balls and other goods from repurposed seat leather is just one way Southwest is reducing waste, protecting the environment, and creating opportunities in communities worldwide.

With the support of Senior Leadership and the help of the Supply Chain Management Department, Southwest identified programs that could use the material to train young adults such as Robinson to convert the materials into shoes, soccer balls, backpacks, keychains, and other leather goods. Robinson had joined a gang when he was 16 but was able to turn his life around when his uncle brought him to Life Beads, one of Southwest's Partner organizations, where he learned leather-working skills.

In addition to Life Beads, other Partners, including SOS Children's Villages and shoemaker Maasai Treads, get the finished products to people in need, such as James, who, with his new pair of shoes, was able to return to school.

In addition to materials from the interiors of its aircraft, Southwest recycles everything it can from old aircraft that it can't resell. About 85 percent of the material in a retired aircraft can be repurposed.

By the spring of 2020, Southwest, through the Repurpose with Purpose program and with the help of Partner organizations, had recycled or reused more than 1 million pounds of discarded materials into useful products. The program is based on one simple idea: Used does not mean useless.

Five hundred leather seat covers will make almost 2,000 pairs of shoes or 1,000 soccer balls for kids.

With the success of LUV Seat, Southwest expanded the program, known as Repurpose with Purpose, and by 2017, it had donated an additional 675,000 pounds of seat covers and other discarded materials. Some of that material went to benefit women in indigenous communities in Mexico, who converted it into sellable goods.

Other materials went to Rethreaded, a program that gives career opportunities to women who are recovering from the trauma of human trafficking. The women use the materials to make fashion jewelry and accessories that Rethreaded sells on its website. The Company also donated materials to the Arise Veterans Foundation, which is using them in rehabilitation programs to help veterans develop entrepreneurial skills.

↑
In 2017, Southwest expanded its Repurpose with Purpose program, an initiative that recycles hundreds of thousands of pounds of discarded material into useful products with the help of Partner organizations.

←
Seat leather that would have been thrown away is turned into sellable goods.

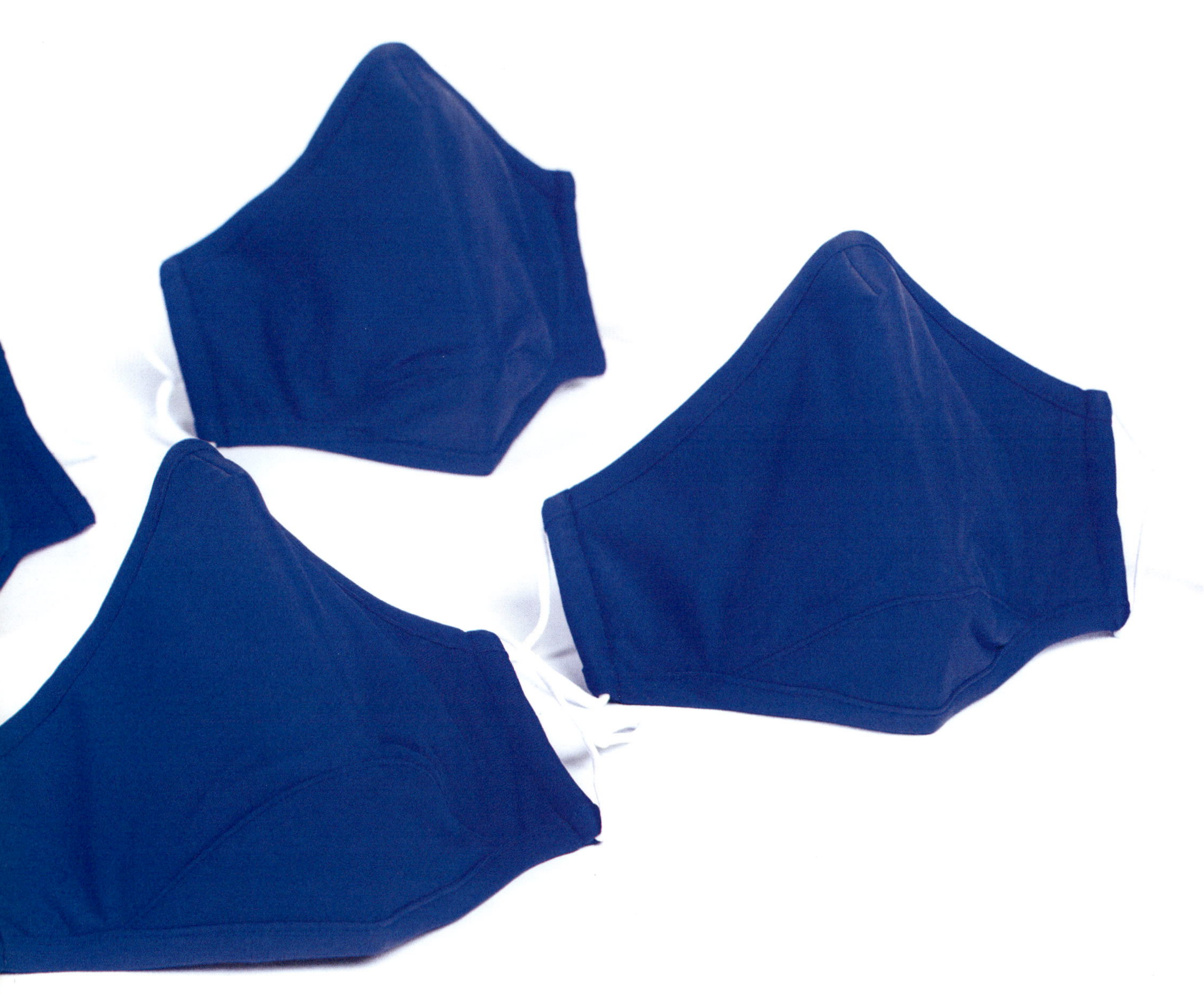

Flying Through a Pandemic

As the coronavirus outbreak spread, Southwest Employees pulled together to fight for the airline's survival, just like they did in its earliest days.

The COVID-19 pandemic greatly affected the commercial aviation industry in 2020. With millions of people infected worldwide, many nations severely restricted travel, and people simply stopped flying. Domestic air travel fell to levels not seen since the 1970s, tumbling some 70 percent from the previous year.

"It's really bad," Southwest Chairman and CEO Gary Kelly told Employees in an October 2020 address. "Costs and spending have been cut dramatically at Southwest, but not nearly enough to offset a 70 percent revenue loss. We would have to wipe out a large swath of salaries, wages, and benefits to match the low traffic levels to have any hope of just breaking even."

The Company had a pandemic response plan that it created in 2007 and updated after other pandemics such as H1N1 and SARS. And while those years of preparation paid off in terms of making decisions and pulling Teams together, COVID presented a challenge the likes of which most companies, including Southwest, had never encountered.

↑
A First Officer wears a mask as part of the Southwest Promise in May 2020.

"Nothing from any of those past events, I think, could prepare us for what COVID has been," said Senior Director Preparedness Karie Lardon. "It impacted every aspect of our business. The number of changes that were needed on the fly, making quick decisions, and putting things in place that we have not had to for past pandemics, was very eye-opening. I have never been a part of a response that has had the same duration and impact that this has."

With the first reports of possible cases in the U.S. in January 2020, Southwest pulled together a Disaster Response Team. It began implementing its plan, canceling nonessential face-to-face meetings, coordinating with the Centers for Disease Control (CDC), and meeting with health organizations to change processes and procedures to support the well-being of Employees and Customers.

Internally, that required quick adjustments. Southwest Airlines University, which provides training for all Employees, canceled in-person classes and, like many public schools and universities around the country, switched to a virtual learning platform that was launched within a matter of days.

The Company also adopted the Southwest Promise, which explained the changes Southwest made to its operations and procedures to support the well-being and comfort of Employees and Customers, including cleaning procedures, physical distancing measures, and mask requirements.

Throughout its response to the pandemic, Southwest continued to evaluate its policies and procedures based on public health guidance, scientific research, and advice from medical and aviation organizations. Gary issued more than 70 video messages, providing transparent updates on the situation to Employees and Customers, and explaining the reasons behind new business decisions and operating procedures the Company adopted.

As the crisis worsened, Gary and other named Executive Officers volunteered to have their base salaries reduced, and the Members of the Board voluntarily reduced their cash retainer fees. The Company offered voluntary separation packages and extended time off to Employees.

Meanwhile, Employees redoubled their efforts to cut expenses, and the Company tried new revenue-generating ideas, such as offering cargo-only charter flights as an on-demand service for the first time in its history as well as significantly increasing charter flights utilizing idle aircraft.

"Our Southwest Warriors have done everything that we asked, and you all have performed magnificently," Gary said. "You are our heroes."

For a generation of Southwest Employees who joined the company after the 9/11 terror attacks in 2001, it was a chance for them to show the same Warrior Spirit that got the Company through earlier crises. "The last couple of months have been different than any other time period that we've ever experienced, and I think it's really shown the grit of the Company and the individual Employees," said Jeremy Ramirez, a 10-year Southwest Employee who works in Network Planning.

"We've circled the wagons, and we're all in this collective mindset of, 'Hey, let's do what we got to do to survive,' and we are going to make it through."

Employees pulled together, once again doing whatever needed to be done, regardless of their job descriptions—emulating a work ethic exemplified by Herb.

They knew they couldn't rest on their laurels. Everyone worked hard to ensure the Southwest legacy endured.

Even as the effects of the pandemic wore on, Southwest continued to add new cities—"We're playing offense," Gary said—reinstating service in 2021 to George Bush Intercontinental Airport in Houston after a 16-year absence and Jackson-Medgar Wiley Evers International Airport in Mississippi after a seven-year absence; as of mid-2021, initiating service to new destinations, a list that, as of mid-2021, included Miami; Palm Springs, Calif.; Steamboat Springs, Colo.; Montrose (Telluride/Crested Butte), Colo.; Chicago (O'Hare); Sarasota/Bradenton, Fla.; Colorado Springs, Colo.; Savannah/Hilton Head; Santa Barbara, Calif.; Fresno, Calif.; Destin/Ft. Walton Beach, Fla.; Myrtle Beach, S.C.; and Bozeman, Mont.; and announcing the intent to serve additional destinations later in 2021, including Eugene, Ore.; Bellingham, Wash.; and Syracuse, N.Y.

In his October 2020 message to Employees, Gary invoked the "spirit of 1972," when everyone at the Company pulled together and invented the 10-Minute Turn to keep the airline flying in the face of adversity.

"You all have done a heroic job in the most challenging of times," he said. "I could not be more proud of you. Don't give up now. Don't ever give up. You've worked too hard, you persevered. We can fight our way through this. We can save every job. Fifty years from now, they'll look back and they'll say, 'Those Employees of 2020, they were really something. They saved Southwest Airlines, and they saved each other's jobs. And truly, that was Southwest's finest hour.'"

Acknowledgments

Thanks to members of the Southwest Airlines 50th Anniversary Team, who dedicated themselves to celebrating this incredible Company milestone (despite the challenges of 2020-2021) and who championed the creation of this book as a shining tribute to Southwest's history for readers to enjoy for years to come. Planning & Delivery Lead Avery Leal deserves special thanks for shepherding the book's process all along the way!

Southwest Creative Studio Senior Photographer Stephen M. Keller contributed his original photography for each of the 50 objects featured in this book, and Southwest Creative Studio Designer Brianna Juda styled each object for photography. Their talents beautifully showcased these iconic objects from Southwest's history. Additional thanks goes to the full Southwest Creative Studio Team, which contributed several of the other photographs throughout this book, giving readers a special look "behind the curtain" at Southwest Airlines.

This book wouldn't have been possible without Richard West, Southwest's Corporate Historian, who uncovered historical details and incredible images from our past, sourced many of the historical objects from the Corporate Archive, and spent hours relentlessly researching Southwest's incredible story. Because of you, Richard, our past will receive the celebration it deserves and will be preserved for the future.

Without Loren Steffy of 30 Point Strategies and the incredible team at History Factory, this book quite literally would never have come to life. Loren, you authentically captured the Southwest voice, and thanks to you, our stories will have an impact into our next 50 years and beyond. History Factory, you brought the vision of a Southwest history book from an idea on paper to reality and designed a masterpiece of which we can be very proud.

And finally, thanks to our Partners at HALO Branded Solutions who made it possible to get this book into the hands of Southwest Employees, Customers, friends, and more.

Index

Page numbers in **bold** indicate illustrations.

D

G

H

L

M

N

O

P

Q

R

S

T

U

V

W

Y